TOUGH SELLING FOR TOUGH TIMES

BY MURRAY RAPHEL AND NEIL RAPHEL

TOUGH SELLING FOR TOUGH TIMES

Copyright © 1992 by Murray and Neil Raphel

Cover design by: Donna Huyett/Studio 151

Manufactured in the United States of America

ISBN 0-9623808-1-9

Library of Congress Catalog Number 91-091251

To: Adrienne
          Anna
          Bennett
          Caroline
          Daniel
          David
          Will

The next generation is our inspiration.

Murray and Neil Raphel

TABLE OF CONTENTS

CHAPTER   PAGE

FOREWORD   vii
  By Robert O. Aders, president
  Food Marketing Institute

INTRODUCTION   1

1. LISTEN!   9
  Interview: **Joe Sugarman**   24

2. SELL!   39
  Interview: **Reese Palley**   52

3. WOW!   63
  Interview: **Stew Leonard**   71

4. HELP!   85
  Interview: **Sol Price**   95

5. REWARD!   105
  Interview: **Tony Ingleton**   118

6. ORGANIZE!   123
  Interview: **Tom Haggai**   138

7. COMPETE!   149
  Interview: **Victor Niederhoffer**   163

8. SURVIVE!   175
  Interview: **Eddy Boas**   185
  Interview: **Eric Lutz**   191

CONCLUSION   197

FOREWORD

It was the best of times, it was the worst of times . . .

So Charles Dickens begins *A Tale of Two Cities*, and so Murray and Neil Raphel demonstrate in this book how businesses can not only survive the most miserable economic conditions, but flourish.

Any mention of tough times conjures up images of the Great Depression, business failures, bread lines and homelessness. Yet other images are as bright as these are dreary. A great innovation in retailing was born in those dark days.

Less than a year after Black Thursday in Jamaica, New York, Michael Cullen opened his first King Kullen, "The World's Most Daring Price Wrecker" — an experiment in mass merchandising that gave birth to the modern supermarket. His success lured more entrepreneurs into the business, and soon consumers from coast to coast benefited from the supermarket — the institution that has done as much as any other to improve the standard of living in the western world.

These entrepreneurs were brash. They were bold. They combined show business and marketing. They knew how to romance the customer with variety and value, economy and convenience. They elected "not to participate" in the depression. They were too busy having fun and tailoring their businesses to consumer needs.

They were a lot like Murray Raphel. Murray himself has operated a retail business in tough times, and he knows firsthand that the burdens of operating in a weak economy are great — but they are often overrated. And Murray also knows that there are many kinds of tough times besides business recessions: changing neighborhoods, natural disasters or brand new competitors opening up down the street.

During the tough times, many businesses fail to observe the fundamentals of good marketing — often because they are distracted by or obsessed with their problems. This book is an excellent guide to those fundamentals, how to sell, sizzle, compete, organize, help, reward and survive — all of it oriented toward the biggest contributor to the bottom line: the consumer. The lessons are timeless, as effective for the tough times as the not-so-tough ones.

Tough Selling for Tough Times is especially compelling for its blend of experience and journalism. Murray draws upon a vast repository of experience, anecdotes, jokes, fables, proverbs, telling details and imparts a great deal of wisdom — both his own and that from the thousands of people encountered on his self-made yellow brick road.

I first met Murray Raphel in his family store in Gordon's Alley in the early '70s. The "Alley" was an inner city shopping mall developed by Murray and his family in pre-casino Atlantic City — and it was thriving in those "tough times." On a counter in Gordon's was Murray's new book, *The Great Brain Robbery*. I read it and instantly realized that the supermarket industry needed Murray Raphel.

Each year in Chicago, the Food Marketing Institute (FMI) holds a supermarket convention and educational exposition, and I wanted Murray to highlight our program of educational workshops at the next show. He liked the idea and the rest is history. Each year since then, he has been the star of the show. In 1986 the FMI Board of Directors honored Murray as the "FMI Superstar of the Decade." The inscription on the plaque went on to say: "In celebration of 10 consecutive all-star performances at the annual convention of the Food Marketing Institute." It then listed the presentation titles, noting that each "was the highest rated show at these FMI conventions, outperforming a total of 512 workshops presented during the decade." Since then, Murray's program has ranked the best of the some 60 workshops given each year. Perhaps "workshop" understates the scope of what Murray does. This year's multimedia presentation was done in six languages to an audience of more than 2,000.

His audience of supermarket executives — all experts in one of the most competitive forms of consumer marketing — could hardly be more discerning. Still, Murray finds the material and manner of presentation that leave them shaking their heads with wonder as they leave Chicago's Arie Crown Theatre. The same phenomenon occurs at other FMI conferences, such as our Pacific Rim convention in Sydney, Australia, our annual General Merchandise and Health and Beauty Aids show, and at numerous regional and state grocery conventions throughout the country.

FMI and the supermarket industry have also benefited from the talents of Murray's family, including his wife, Ruth, and son, Neil. Besides coauthoring this book, Neil has served as editor of *foodmarketing*, FMI's quarterly newsletter celebrating the best in supermarket marketing, advertising and promotions.

Yes, Murray knows the supermarket industry, and the supermarket industry knows Murray Raphel.

The people in the supermarket industry would love to have him all to themselves, but he has shared his special insights with numerous industries, as the examples in this book demonstrate. And that is in the best interests of the consumer.

If you have noticed significant improvements in the way supermarkets sell their products and services — more passion and pizazz, a more focused message, a stronger sense of community and consumer awareness — Murray deserves a large measure of the credit. Thank you, Murray!

Robert O. Aders
Washington DC
September 1991

(Robert O. Aders is president and CEO of the Food Marketing Institute, a nonprofit association representing 1,500 grocery retailers and wholesalers in the United States and 60 other nations. Its members account for over half of all U.S. grocery sales.)

PREFACE

This book is about overcoming "tough times." Tough times can certainly come in the guise of an economic recession. But just as devastating can be a competitor opening a new store just down the street. Or a key employee getting sick. Or a bank refusing to extend a loan. Or a flood destroying your inventory.

This book is about the "tough" selling steps that you can use to achieve business success. It is about business people who have used these methods to overcome adversity. Each chapter contains stories, quotes, interviews, anecdotes and advice. Each chapter focuses on a different characteristic of business success. It is a program you can use today. In your business.

Overcoming "tough times" begins with your mental attitude.

Example: We asked a number of successful business people how they were altering their business practices during the recent recession. Their surprising answers ranged from, "What recession?" to "I'm doing what I've always done — making my customers happy" to "I'm not planning any reductions." We especially enjoyed Sam Walton's remark when asked about how he was planning to respond to the recession. Walton replied, "We decided not to participate."

The purpose of this book is not to champion a Pollyannish view of the world or your business. The book's point is best expressed by supermarket owner Stew Leonard when writing about tough times — "We've all had tough times at one time or another. But the secret is to put them behind us."

So read on and discover the business solution to your personal "tough times."

INTRODUCTION QUOTES

George Bernard Shaw, 1893 — "People are always blaming their circumstances for what they are. I don't believe in circumstances. The people who get on in this world are the people who get up and look for the circumstances they want, and, if they can't find them, make them."

Stew Leonard, supermarket owner, Norwalk, Connecticut — Is now a tough time for retailers? "No. It never is a tough time. If you believe times are tough, times will be tough . . . As long as people are going to eat and breathe and live, they're going to have to spend money. And as long as they're going to spend money, our job is simply to give them what they want. We've all had tough times at one time or another, but the secret is to put them behind us."

Victor Niederhoffer, commodities trader, New York City — "One of the things that I do at a time like the present is to allocate my resources where they have the highest return. A mistake many businesses make in difficult times is to concentrate on loss prevention and crisis management. What I've tried to do with most of my businesses, most of my activities, is to be diverse enough so that they'll always be some activity where there's room for expansion, where the capital investments have good returns."

Sol Price, founder, Price Club — "We look upon the recession as a problem but also as an opportunity. The depressed real estate market provides us with unique opportunities to acquire land at substantially lower prices than would have been the case a couple of years ago."

Tom Haggai, CEO, IGA Food Stores — "There is a rule of thumb that I use: You economize for efficiency, but you have to sell for prosperity. I've always had people much older than I as advisors. Without exception, they told me they made their best business decisions in tough times. Not their best profits, but their best decisions. And they never let tough times keep them from having a strategy for progress. In fact, the tough times help them prioritize what they're doing and eliminate programs that are no longer productive. Recession, then, becomes preparation time to take greater advantage than your competition of the recovery."

RECENT "TOUGH TIMES" HEADLINES

Dun & Bradstreet — The number of U.S. business failures jumped 20 percent to over 60,000 in 1990 — the sharpest annual increase since 1983 — and the pace has continued into 1991.

July 29, 1991 issue of Fortune magazine — In an article titled "Winning Over The New Consumer," the author comments, "A remarkable 23 percent of department store sales in the U.S. are being rung up in outlets that are currently in bankruptcy." One point made in the article: Consumers are retreating from a 1980s mindset of buying quality at any price. Now consumers have a recession philosophy. They want value, quality goods at reasonable prices.

Subhead from a January 6, 1991 New York Times article — "In a recession, adaptability may be a company's most valuable commodity." Law firms are moving into new fields like bankruptcy and environmental law. Berkeley Caterers in New York City is now renting party equipment to customers who want to put on a party themselves. A large accounting firm is now emphasizing consulting services in cost containment, capital raising and credit.

1990 New Yorker Christmas cartoon — Father to young boy waiting for Santa Claus — "When he comes down the chimney, ask him if he wants to buy our house."

THE CHICKEN LITTLE STORY

Chicken Little was scared.

There she was relaxing in the hen house when suddenly an acorn fell on her head. She panicked and ran around screaming,"The sky is falling down! The sky is falling down!"

She decided to go to the King and tell him the news. On the way she met Henny Penny, Ducky Lucky, Goosey Lucey and Turkey Lurkey. She told them, "Haven't you heard the news? The sky is falling down. I'm on my way to tell the King!"

They were running down the road and Foxy Loxy stopped to ask them what was happening. "The sky is falling down!" they screamed.

"This is an emergency," said Foxy. "Quick, jump into my truck and I'll take you to the king!"

He said he would house them in his home until the trouble passed. As he was driving his captives to his home, another acorn fell from the sky and hit Foxy on the head. He ran from the truck and yelled, "The sky is falling! The sky is falling down!"

It was then that Chicken Little saw the acorn, went back to the hen house and planted it next to her coop.

Years later when the acorn grew into a giant oak tree she would tell her children about the time The Sky Was Falling Down.

Almost.

Today there are Chicken Little's running around the world again screaming in the language of their country, "The sky is falling down!" And, at first glance it seems it very well may be. Consider the evidence:

• Dozens of life insurance companies in North America failed last year. Startling news for businesses considered recession-proof.

• Many savings and loans went bankrupt and even the largest banks in the U.S. are having difficult financial problems.

• Commercial real estate is in its worst state in many decades.

Business is tough. And getting tougher.

But there are successful entrepreneurs around the world posting substantial increases and record bottom line profits!

How can this be? What are the reasons some succeed when others fail?

TRAVELING DOWN ROUTE 53

Separated by a short stretch of Route 53 in tree-shrouded southeastern Connecticut are the homes of two fascinating entrepreneurs.

Near the east end of Norwalk is a sprawling farmlike edifice which houses the busiest retail establishment in the world, Stew

Leonard's. Stew Leonard's supermarket does more than $100,000,000 worth of business at a single location, with five million shoppers passing through its doors every year. **Stew Leonard's does more business per square foot than any other retail establishment in the world.**

Stew Leonard's supermarket is a mini-Disneyland, with dancing mechanical milk cartons, a petting zoo and the freshest, tastiest, largest assortment of meats, cheeses, baked goods, fruits, vegetables and groceries you can imagine.

And countless times per day, team members (not "employees") trek through the one wide aisle which makes up Stew Leonard's. The team members are looking for trash on the floor, are straightening merchandise, are making certain the food is "piled high," making sure all their customers are **satisfied** customers.

Stew Leonard tells visitors he wants to make twenty nickels, not one dollar. He wants volume, and he wants to offer the best products at the lowest possible prices. Stew Leonard wants to make shopping an entertaining experience. And the shoppers who cram their cars into his three vast parking lots are ample evidence that he is succeeding in his desire to do more business.

Just north on Route 53 are the rolling hills of Weston, Connecticut where Victor Niederhoffer's imposing house stands. Victor's Weston home is a retreat from Manhattan, where Victor battles the commodities markets and looks for opportunities in his merger and acquisition business.

Victor invites us to a relaxing weekend in the country. After losing at squash, racquetball, tennis, chess, checkers and even being outwitted at repartee, we are allowed to leave. By the way, Victor was North American squash champion for 14 years. He is not inclined to lose in any enterprise he sets his will to.

We often travel the Norwalk to Weston route because Stew and Victor are great friends of ours. And as our car winds up the hills of Route 53, we think about our two friends. Their personalities are very different. Stew wants to serve the public, satisfy the public, make the public enjoy shopping with him.

Victor wants to win. He enjoys and excels at games but has to end up on top.

Is there a unifying force between our entrepreneur friends in Connecticut? How about the other successful entrepreneurs we have met in our journeys? What are the success factors that make these individuals stand out from the pack and make their businesses work so well?

In this book we discuss eight success characteristics. We have included interviews with business people like Victor Niederhoffer and Stew Leonard who best exemplify these characteristics.

Here is an outline of these success characteristics:

1. Listen! (Wants and Needs)— the discerning of customers wants and needs. The ability to test before doing, try before committing.

2. Sell! (Promotional Ideas) — every time two people meet, a sale is made. The best business people know how to make purchasing decisions seem like an opportunity for their customers.

3. Wow! (Enthusiasm) — the ability to excite colleagues and customers about your products and services.

4. Help! (Customer Service) — the recognition that the customer is the life blood of a business and must be coddled, entertained and rewarded.

5. Reward! (Customer Retention) — the knowledge that your best customers are current customers and not future prospects, and that your best customers should be constantly rewarded.

6. Organize! (Self Discipline) — the ability to organize your life before you approach the public with your ideas.

7. Compete! (Self Confidence) — the fierce desire to be number one, or, the best you can be. The inability to settle for second best.

8. Survive! (Hard Work) — top business people firmly believe that success is more perspiration than inspiration and that what you get out of the bottom line is what you put into it.

By understanding these success principles, you will be prepared to withstand any "tough times" in your business.

TOUGH SELLING FOR TOUGH TIMES

1

LISTEN!

LISTEN! INTRODUCTION

Do you listen to your customers? **Really** listen?

If you're not listening **actively** to your customers, you are headed for disaster in the marketplace.

The very first step in Tough Selling is to assess your customers' wants and needs. In the 1990s you are going to have to move beyond *customer service* to *customer satisfaction*. But you cannot satisfy your customers until you are absolutely sure of what they want.

Here is a tour through the world of listening. You will learn how outstanding corporations and merchants keep ahead of the competition by keeping up to date with their customers.

At the conclusion of the chapter is the story of entrepreneur Joe Sugarman. Joe always keeps both ears firmly attuned to the marketplace and is often at the cutting edge of new consumer products. Read how Joe created a national market for the BluBlocker sunglasses and **listen** to his advice for getting into synch with your customers.

Hear today. Otherwise, your customers may be gone tomorrow.

LISTEN! QUOTES

Novelist and philosopher Andre Gide once opened a lecture by noting, "All this has been said before, but since nobody listened, it must be said again."

Psychiatrist walking down the street. Another psychiatrist passes and says, "Good morning." First pyschiatrist says to himself, "I wonder what he meant by **that**?"

"You can't fake listening. It shows." — **Racquel Welch**

LISTEN! FACTS

 • The average person spends 70 percent of their waking day in some form of communications process: 9 percent writing, 16 percent reading, 30 percent talking and **45 percent listening**.

- A message heard only one time is 66 2/3 percent forgotten within 24 hours and 90 percent forgotten within 30 days.
- The average rate of speech is about 125 words a minute; the average person thinks at a rate nearly four times faster.

(Listening facts from Ed Kelsay, attorney, Oklahoma City and Royal Bank of Canada newsletter)

A QUIZ TO READ OUT LOUD TO A FRIEND OF YOURS

Imagine you're a bus driver heading north. You drive 4 miles north, then you drive 3 miles south, then you drive 2 miles east and then you drive 1 mile west. Those are the facts. Now the question. How old is the bus driver?*

ACTIVE LISTENING

Here's the basic rule in selling:

Find out what your customers want to buy and give it to them.

The problem is we are so busy talking all the time we do not take the time to listen. And if we do **not** listen, we cannot find out what our customers want.

Very few people listen . . . actively. Educator Mortimer Adler says that listening is not a passive activity. You must listen with your mind as well as your ear. "Your job is to reach out and catch what is in the mind of the speaker — just as the catcher in a baseball game must actively stretch for the ball the pitcher has just thrown."

Tom Peters in an interview in Hyatt Magazine pointed out three characteristics of successful business listening:

1. Listening with intensity. Why not give out your home phone number?
2. Spend time "hanging out" in the marketplace.
3. Take what you hear seriously and act fast.

---

* If your friend is like most of us, she will focus on the total mileage instead of the word **you**. The question is: How old are you?

Listening is a two-way street. When you talk to someone, try to frame your speech in a way that makes for easy listening. Dr. Jesse Nirenberg, a New York psychologist, made the following suggestions for holding a person's attention:

• Always start with the conclusion — never with a question.

• Do not lead to your main idea slowly. If you do, the listener's mind might have skipped ahead of you.

• Translate what you have to say into potential benefits.

• Avoid pronouns. Instead of "What do you think of this?" say, "What do you think of (something specific)?"

• Get feedback by asking your listeners questions.

A SUPER MARKETER

We once visited Stew Leonard, owner of the world's most successful supermarket in Norwalk, Connecticut. (See interview with Stew at end of "Wow!" chapter). The purpose of our visit was to find out why he did more than $100 million a year in **one** supermarket, the largest volume of any supermarket in the world. Aren't all supermarkets alike? Don't they all sell food? What made his different?

The day we arrived he had flowers on sale in the front of the store as an experiment. As customers made purchases, Stew would talk to them and ask them questions:

"Do you like the selection?"

"Are the prices OK?"

"Would you rather buy one dozen or half a dozen?"

"How about plants? Do you think we should carry plants?"

"What kind of plants do you think we should carry?"

"How much would you pay for them?"

Each conversation lasted just a few minutes. He spoke with a dozen people and all the time he was asking the customers their preference, a young man, off to the side, quietly listening, was jotting down their answers. Stew walked over to him and said, "Have my secretary type up those notes and give them to the buyer."

Stew came back to me and said, "I've never understood what the fuss was all about in doing research and surveys and hiring planners. All I do is ask my customers what they want to buy . . . and then give it to them."

CORPORATE LISTENING

Listening is the most used communication skill but the least taught.

Some major corporations are learning this. Look at their ads in national magazines:

"Before we designed the BMC computers,we listened."
   —BMC division of Technology Group

"We hear you. We're doing a lot of listening these days at P & G."
   —Procter & Gamble

"When you told us nobody could understand your business like people in your business, we listened."
   —Unisys

Unless you take the time to listen, you cannot communicate. General Electric sent a survey to purchasing agents to find out why they were losing sales. More than 75 percent gave the same answer: "Your salesmen talk too much. . ."

"The bad salesman has an inability to listen," says Curtis Berrien, senior vice president of Forum Company of Boston, a firm that specializes in management and sales training. "He is pushy. He talks all the time. He talks technical characteristics of the product rather than the benefits."

Ralph Cornider, vice president of marketing and sales for GE in the 1950s, recognized this problem but few listened to him at that time. The tactic of big business was to develop a new idea, make it and then give it to the salesmen to sell. Cornider said the order was wrong. It should be reversed: "First," he said, "look at the market. Then determine what's needed in that market. And **then** have it made."

But that was revolutionary thinking in the 50s. It was a simple idea, but it was too radical for most firms to accept.

One way you you find out "what's needed" is to simply ask. **Try customer focus groups.** Management needs to meet with customers on a regular basis asking, "What do you like? What don't you like?" They find most customers have the same compliments and complaints. By listening they can eliminate the latter. When Feargal Quinn, owner of Superquinn supermarkets in Ireland meets with his Customer Council — made up of people who shop his supermarket — he begins the sessions with "Don't tell me what you **like** about our store. Let's talk about what you **don't like**. What you want us to do differently."

When people (or companies) listen, the results are often dramatic.

Polaroid embossed a toll free 800 number on their cameras. They asked the customer to call if she had a problem with Polaroid film or cameras. The first year they had nearly 300,000 phone calls.

Problem: "The film rips when I pull it out of the camera."

Solution: Design the camera so you simply press the button and the picture comes out automatically.

Problem: "The picture didn't develop properly." When Polaroid asked, "Did you change the batteries?" the customer answered, "Batteries? What batteries? Does the camera have batteries?"

Solution: Include batteries with **each** package of film.

Polaroid was asking for trouble but ended up with satisfied customers because they listened.

WHY WAS THIS MAN SO POPULAR?

A hostess once invited a certain man to all her parties. Everyone would tell her later how much they enjoyed being in his company. The hostess was mystified. The man was no life of the party. He was in fact, quiet and subdued. What quality did he have that she missed?

At the next party she introduced him to a guest and then hovered nearby to hear his technique. It was very simple. After being introduced to a stranger he would say, "Tell me something about yourself. . ." And then he just . . . listened.

He listened to people talk about themselves. He encouraged them to tell him about their jobs, their family, their hopes, their dreams. How they arrived at their present station in life. Where would they like to go on their next vacation. Why? For how long?

Later everyone told the hostess what a marvelous addition he was to the party.

Why? Because people who listen seem to care more, seem more open minded and concerned. Those who continually talk come across as pompous, self-centered and narrow-minded. They interrupt and they criticize. They earn a bad and sometimes undeserved reputation.

LISTENING TO WHAT SOMEONE WEARS

Unisys runs listening seminars. They teach sales people and management how-to-listen.

"Listening" Unisys says, "is more than hearing. It's our primary method of receiving information." Unisys points out that people hear words but rarely listen for the meaning of the words.

If you "listen well" you not only hear the sounds of words but you also see the physical movement of people when they talk. You hear their voice tone. You see their body movement. You notice the way they wear their clothes. What you hear, what you see, are physical processes that can be improved with training.

You have to listen with more than your ears. People give out signs when they talk. The look on their face. The way they stand. Their gestures, pauses, hesitations. All this body language can often tell you more about what the person says or means than spoken language.

Folded arms usually means they have made up their mind and you can't convince them otherwise. If the person you are talking to keeps on looking around the room, you have lost their attention. The old glancing at the watch routine means they are bored and looking for a way to escape. There are lots of tell-tale signs, but you have to watch for them. Body language is important because every little movement has a meaning all its own.

GOOD LISTENING = MOTIVATION

Educator Mortimer Adler was asked if there is one thing that would make all of us better listeners.

He replied, "Motivation. If someone says to you, 'Shall I tell you why I love you?' or, 'We're thinking of promoting you to Vice President' you stop daydreaming and really listen to what that person has to say."

All of us are in the business of communication. Though we all speak the same language, it is amazing how difficult it is to understand one another. If you have a business and someone calls for an item and you do not listen carefully to nuances, phrases, exact information, you wind up apologizing, rewriting, apologizing, remaking, apologizing, etc . . .

Are there ways we can make sure what we say is accurately read, accurately heard and actually acted upon?

Sure. Here are four guidelines to follow:

1. **Listen to what your customer is saying.**
2. **Practice listening.**
3. **Accept new ideas.**
4. **Respond appropriately.**

1. LISTEN TO WHAT YOUR CUSTOMER IS SAYING.

Remember Norman Rockwell's famous front page of faces for the Saturday Evening Post called "Gossip"? It began with one person telling a secret to someone else. It was repeated person to person until it returned to the first person with a message entirely unrelated to the one she gave originally.

David Ogilvy, advertising guru, tells the story of the English major in World War I who sent a verbal message back from the front line trenches to division headquarters. The message was: "Send up reinforcements. We are going to advance." By the time it was repeated mouth-to-mouth through all the levels, it finally reached headquarters as, "Send up three and four pence. We are going to a dance."

You can learn to listen by watching others listen. A good place to start: your TV. The movie theater. The stage. See how the actors "listen" to other actors. When the talker talks, the listenee listens. (Some actors wind up stealing the scene because they are such good listeners.)

Direct marketing experts "listen" by testing their products. If they send 10,000 advertisements to customers and only 100 answer they see only one percent are "listening." They quickly change tactics and techniques to build a larger audience.

Book of the Month Club started by **not** giving the customer a choice for the monthly selection. Customers wrote and complained. Said they wanted options not just **one** choice. The club changed to what the customer wanted.

If you are not listening, you are encouraging the customer to leave you. A Neilsen survey showed small problems that only cost a few dollars or result in a minor inconvenience will have only one person in 50 complain. How about the remaining 49 who don't take the time to complain? Do they stop shopping with your business or stop buying your product? Probably.

Encourage your customers to complain.

If it is true that most customers will **not** complain (and it is) and you can convince them you are really listening and not just running ads saying you do, they will remain as loyal customers.

Here's why: If your customer is happy, she will tell three other people how great you are.

If your customer is unhappy, she will tell eleven other people how terrible you are.

With odds like that, you don't to have to worry about stocking merchandise for next season. If your customer is unhappy, you won't be in business.

How do you have people tell you their problems? Join the AAA. Not the automobile club but the Ask/ Answer/ Analyze club.

• **Ask:** "If you're mad, call John" was the headline of a bank ad in Minneapolis. They hired someone whose sole job was to handle complaints. They repeated the ad two years later with a new headline: "Since we ran this ad two years ago, we've had nothing but trouble. Thank you!"

They received 2,500 concerns, complaints and questions. Result: They identified problems that existed but were not seen.

• **Answer:** It's one thing to ask, "What's wrong?" It's a greater step to do something. Call. Apologize. Explain why you charge for gift wrapping. Or gift cards. Or delivery. Or why the alterations promised were not ready. Or the signed deal **not** on their desk at 9 AM as promised. Act on what went wrong and why. Make a list to find who is complaining about what? How often. Keep track of what customers write you after you answer them. (Great testimonials)

• **Analyze.** Were the original complaints taken care of? How long did it take? Ask others in your business how they would handle the same problem.

In this day of Tough Selling, the consumer feels all stores look alike or all businesses are the same. **But,** you are different if you're the one that cares about—**really cares about** your customers by simply listening to what they want.

2. PRACTICE LISTENING.

Listening can become habit forming. Start today by forcing yourself to completely listen, **really listen**, to whatever anyone is talking to you about. Look them in the eye. Hear them out. Concentrate. There is an old Welsh proverb that says it well, "He understands badly who listens badly."

Dan Fazenden, president of Roger Fazenden Realty in Minneapolis, uses a "Plan to Report" technique. He says, "When someone tells you something, listen so intently that you could report it almost verbatim to someone else."

If you are not sure you understand what was said, say so.

"Does that mean . . . ?"

"Is this what you're saying . . . ?"

This shows you really **are** listening. Ernest Hemingway, known for his realistic dialogue, repeated conversations he had heard. He said, "When people talk, listen completely. Most people never listen."

Listening is anticipation. Know what you are going to say or do before you say or do it. See if you can become like the waiter who fills the glass of water before you ask or has the match lit when you take out a cigarette. This instinct for knowing the right word or phrase or movement is developed through proper listening.

One night, before a major battle, the Duke of Marlboro was reconnoitering the terrain facing the enemy and dropped his glove. Cadogan, his chief of staff, dismounted and gave it back.

Later that evening, Marlboro spoke to Cadogan outlining his battle plans for the next day saying, "Put a battery of guns where I dropped my glove."

Said Cadogan, "I have already done so, sir."

There was no need to communicate. He learned to "listen" through years of being together.

Listening is concentration.

A study by J. Walter Thompson questioned 100 viewers of the TV miniseries, "The Winds of War."

The study showed 19 percent of the viewers recalled commercials from Volkswagon, 32 percent remembered Kodak, 32 percent Prudential, 28 percent Budweiser, 18 percent American Express and 26 percent Mobil.

Ready for the punch line? Here it is: **None of these companies advertised on the "Winds of War."**

What You Say Is What You Mean. Sometimes.

Verbal language can mean many things to many people. There are more than 14,000 meanings for the 500 most commonly used words in the English language.

We once outfitted a young man in a sport jacket in our store. He admired himself in the mirror and said, "Boy, that's really bad!"

We said fine, we would find something else. Why should he wear something "bad"?

"You don't understand," he said, "It's **really** bad!"

We went from being insulted to being confused to being introduced to the fact that "being bad" really meant, in his vernacular, "really great!"

If you think it is difficult to understand what is meant in conversation, you are not alone. Sometimes we say one thing and mean another. The Greeks had a word for it: "oxymorons" meaning "pointedly foolish."

Oxymorons are quite common today:
- Jumbo shrimp. (How can it be jumbo if it's a shrimp?)
- Realistic estimate. (How can it be realistic if it's an estimate?)
- War games. (If it's war, it ain't a game.)

There's a whole collection in our language including: Congressional ethics. Military intelligence. Open secret. Postal service. Sudden death. Thunderous silence. Plastic glasses. Awfully good.

And those are words in English! Do not feel content simply because there are 386 million people who speak the same English language as you. Remember there are more than one billion who speak Chinese; 600 million, Hindustani; 265 million, Russian; 117 million, Japanese; 245 million, Spanish. Not to mention the millions who speak Tagalog, Turkish or Thai.

Listening in other languages

Imagine the difficulty in translating into English some idiomatic foreign phrases. Some gaffes in the past include:
- When President Carter spoke of "the desire of the Polish people," the Polish translation came out as "lusts of the Polish people."
- Chevrolet advertised their Nova car in Latin America and sales were flat. Reason: No va in Spanish means, "It doesn't go."
- There is an Italian boutique with a sign in English for tourists advertising dresses for "street walking."
- A Paris hotel offers "tea in a bag just like mother."
- Translating the slogan, "Coke adds life" into some Oriental languages had it come out as "bringing your ancestors back from the grave."
- Translating Braniff's promotion for their all leather airline seats into Spanish with the headline "Sentado En Cuero" can be loosely translated as "Sit naked." (An interesting gimmick to increase sales.)

• Then there's the Chinese exporter who tried to market a radio in the U.S. and failed. The brand name: White Elephant.

• Close Up toothpaste's slogan of "put your money where your mouth is" was changed for customers in Zimbabwe to a picture of a fish hook to suggest that Close Up helps someone "hook" their future spouse.

3. ACCEPT NEW IDEAS.

Just because a selling pattern or written copy worked before does not mean it cannot be improved. Watch what's happening in the news to sense a shift in national trends, mores, style.

Niederhoffer and Niederhoffer, a Wall Street commodities firm has outstanding success because they decided **not** to specialize in one commodity as most other experts did.

They spent two years assembling data to show how commodity prices around the world interrelate. Weather conditions on the Falkland Islands can affect the price of wool which can affect the price of gold in Tokyo. They feel they must listen to everything, everyday to continue their record of success. (See interview with Victor Niederhoffer at end of "Compete!" chapter.)

4. RESPOND APPROPRIATELY

A midwestern bank put together a mailing to customers inviting them to the bank's million dollar remodeling party. The brochure spoke of the marble from Italy, the ultrasonic elevators, the new computers, the expensive carpeting. Then someone on the staff asked, "How is the customer helped by us spending their money this way?"

The point: Take all these features and translate them into customer benefits: No long teller lines. Answers on loans in one day or less. Efficient 24 hour banking. Less ego talk. More customer talk. Then customers will listen. Come. Buy.

It also helps the other's person's ability to listen when you tell them what you are going to talk about.

"I know you're a busy person. There are just four things I want to talk about with you today. Here they are." Then list all four. Tell them one at a time. They will listen because they know where you are going and can prepare their answers.

Good listening, like Gaul, is divided into three parts:

A. Interpretation. ("What did they really mean by that?")

B. Evaluation. ("OK, now that I know what they mean, what do I do?")

C. Responding. ("Here's my answer. Now, are **you** listening to me?")

And you must be patient. There are many distractions.

External (Noise, people)

Internal ("Don't confuse me. My mind is already made up.")

Eternal ("Won't he ever stop talking? I've forgotten half of what he said.")

THE REWARDS OF SILENCE

So listen. Very carefully. Starting today. It will result in larger sales, bigger profits, or, at the very least, like our friend earlier, receiving invitations to the best parties in town.

Here is a tip which will help you in future negotiations:

He who talks first, loses.

When you have made your point, shut up!

Think about it. In a situation where you have completed your argument and the customer does not answer, the pressure of silence tempts you to keep on talking. You want to add, "Don't you agree with that?" or "Isn't that a good deal?"

Both of these questions can be answered by the customer very comfortably, easily and naturally with "No."

So finish what you have to say and shut up.

And wait.

And wait.

And wait.

The other person will cough, swallow, look around the room and finally . . . finally give you an answer that more times than not will be exactly what you wanted to hear.

Simply because you decided to listen!

USE THIS CHART TO BECOME AN INSTANT EXPERT IN BUREAUCRESE LANGUAGE

Phil Broughton worked for many years with the U.S. Public Health Service. Every day he would read and hear certain bureaucratic words repeated as if on cue but which had little or no meaning. He accumulated them and divided them into three groups of ten phrases and came up with a technique he calls the **Systematic Buzz Phrase Projector.** Here are the thirty words, each in their own column:

0. Integrated	0. Management	0. Options
1. Total	1. Organizational	1. Flexibility
2. Systematized	2. Monitored	2. Capability
3. Parallel	3. Reciprocal	3. Mobility
4. Functional	4. Digital	4. Programming
5. Responsive	5. Logistical	5. Concept
6. Optional	6. Transitional	6. Time phase
7. Synchronized	7. Incremental	7. Projection
8. Compatible	8. Third-generation	8. Hardware
9. Balanced	9. Policy	9. Contingency.

Here's how it works: Think of any three digit number. Then take the corresponding words from EACH column

For example: the number 736 gives you the Buzz Phrase, "Synchronized reciprocal time phase." Fantastic. You will really impress the team with that one.

Said Broughton: "Nobody will have the remotest idea what you're talking about. But the important thing is that no one is about to admit it."

Which simply goes to prove that few people . . . LISTEN.

INTRODUCTION TO JOE SUGARMAN INTERVIEW

Remember the kids' toys that were popular a few years ago called "transformers"?

The toy looked like a monster from outer space. But tuck in the arms, fold up the legs, and voila!, a race car.

Joe Sugarman is a transformer.

Joe can take a concept which thousands of people have looked at. Then his unique imagination twists the concept into a new shape and thousands of people say, "Why didn't I think of that?"

In 1971, Joe went from running an ad agency to forming a company to market the world's first pocket calculator using direct marketing — all from the basement of his home. His home-spun company soon grew into America's largest single source of space-age products, and Joe introduced new electronic products such as the digital watch and cordless telephones. He also had a few failures (the $1,500 laser beam mouse trap didn't attract a single buyer — or mouse).

In the late 1980s, someone loaned Joe a pair of sunglasses which blocked out blue light and ultraviolet rays. The concept had been around for 50 years, yet represented less than one percent of the market.

Joe liked the product. And because he thought the product was useful for people, he twisted, cajoled, produced, marketed, **transformed** the product into an entire industry!

BluBlocker sunglasses are now a household word. And in searching for new ways to introduce the product, Joe helped create a new industry, the 30 minute infomercial on cable television.

Sugarman describes in this interview how all his successes are fueled by failure. Joe explains how success may be an accident, and failure provides prime learning opportunities. He also shows how his success depends on **listening** to the wants and needs of customers

So, if you've ever been the tiniest bit afraid to try to transfer your dreams into reality, read on. Joe Sugarman will guide you.

JOE SUGARMAN INTERVIEW

Q. How did you get involved with BluBlocker sunglasses?

A. One day I was in LA to look at probably one of the last high tech products that I would try to sell, a portable fax machine. I was driving in a car with the fax machine salesman. As we were driving down the highway the salesman handed me a pair of sunglasses and he said, "Take a look through these sunglasses, and you'll be amazed. Things will appear sharper and clearer."
    The salesman was right.
    A friend of the salesman made the sunglasses and delivered several pairs to me. At the time I was putting out a catalog for United Airlines. I noticed that one of the products that we were going to put in was not available and I thought of the sunglasses. I photographed them and wrote the ad in a day. When I wrote the ad I knew it was a winner. Every once in awhile you just have a strong feeling about a product.
    In addition to just running it in that catalog, I decided to run a few tests in other media. The response rate to this pair of sunglasses was way beyond what I could have ever hoped for or even imagined.
    I realized that I had a very big product on my hands. The BluBlocker concept, that is the concept of blocking blue light, has been around for many many years. Sunglasses to block blue light were used by pilots in the Air Force during World War II, and I suspect after seeing pictures of Lindbergh's sunglasses, that he also used BluBlockers. But nobody had really capitalized on the product, because when I got into the business, BluBlockers represented maybe one percent of the sunglass market in the U.S.
    I immediately contacted factories in the Far East, created my own brand name and developed an ad campaign. I ran a very heavy schedule in every consumer magazine that I could get my hands on and all the airline publications.

Q. So you changed the name of the product?

A. Yes. I came up with the name BluBlocker because it blocked blue light.

One of the things we found out through a lot of research and documentation was the ultraviolet portion of sunlight caused cataracts. There was documentation for that. There was also documentation that blue light caused many eye problems as well. So in our national advertising campaign we emphasized the fact that our product blocked out all of the UV light and the blue light, thereby making it very safe for your eyes. Since the ozone layer is deteriorating quite rapidly, sunglasses are now needed to protect yourself from the sunlight. It is a necessity, a medical requirement.

The ad campaign was extremely successful. Out of 100-150 magazines that we ran it in, I think there was maybe one that did not at least break even. Many were quite profitable.

Then we heard about cable television allowing half hour commercials. I had always been tempted to do cable. I avoided it because I felt I needed a half hour to do a proper sales job, since most of our products were moderately priced to expensive. In order to sell our products I always felt, being a salesman, that I had to have a half hour or at least fifteen minutes, but certainly not just sixty or thirty seconds. When I heard about thirty minute commercials, I decided to take my earnings from the successful print campaign and create a half hour television commercial for BluBlockers.

I hired a producer, hired a media person and went out and created a half hour commercial. It was fairly new advertising medium at the time and we decided to really be creative. We came up with a concept called "Consumer Challenge," which was a board of people who would look over a product and present the pros and cons. Throughout all my advertising career I have presented both the positive and negative aspects of products to present a proper picture to the consumer. We did this in the television commercial. We made it like a consumer program and it ran for approximately two years.

We were one of the early pioneers in this area and that program was very successful. The thirty minute commercial worked very well for us, and, as a result we started to develop our own television programs. However, we ran into a few regulatory problems. The medium was new. There was no regulation on how to present the program. Although we had commercials, the regulatory agencies felt that it was not sufficient that we should have certain disclaimers at the beginning and at the end. They felt the program looked too much like a consumer program and not like an advertisement.

We decided to totally change our concept and came out with an advertisement called, "The making of a commercial." We talked about the fact we were making a commercial. We included disclaimers. It turned out to be a very interesting format and we were able to show a couple new products as well as continuing the sunglass ads.

Although BluBlocker is still our main product, we do have other product lines that we have developed since then, that we put in our catalog. We do catalog mailings and we also do direct mailing. We are also doing direct response radio. We still do print, but very minimally, considerably less than we used to do.

Q. When you first tried on this product and you liked it, could you fathom that you would be where you are today with it?

A. No. All the years we were handling electronics, I was really handling other peoples' products. In addition to that, electronics is the type of industry that if you have a product and it is very hot one minute, three months later it could not only be cold but also obsolete. You really had to be on your toes. I might have had fifty products that I was running concurrently. We had to write an entire ad campaign for each product. We had to investigate each product.

It was not a very easy business. I had always in the back of my mind looked for the opportunity to actually get out of electronics into something that was more stable, and, more importantly, getting into a product that I myself owned.

Something happened once that really convinced me to go into business for myself. A company came to me with a product, a thermostat. They were a very small company. There were only two or three people in the company. They could not sell their thermostat to anyone else. Nobody would consider buying it. It didn't look very good. The company was very small and they were competing against the likes of Honeywell and other very large companies. They came to us and we took on the product and came up with a very unique approach. The product sold exceptionally well for three years. During those three years, the company grew and grew and continued to grow and started to distribute its product in the retail market.

Finally Honeywell bought them out and paid them twenty million dollars. The next thing I know I get a letter from the sales manager thanking us for our past business and saying you can now contact so and so at Honeywell if you want to place future orders. There was never an acknowledgement that the final outcome was a direct result of our efforts. At that point I said, "Why can't we take a product of our own and make it a big product? We've been doing it for many people for many years."

When the sunglasses came out, I saw the success of the initial promotions. I've learned that you wait for a big success before you decide to carve a niche for yourself. We had this big success and it was a matter of sitting down and determining where I was going to buy the product, what I was going to call it and what my strategy would be for the future. That's what I did when I realized that I had a winner.

Q. *Didn't you supply the sunglasses for the Pizza Hut promotion tied to the movie "Back to the Future II"?*

A. Yes, that was an opportunity that I seized.

Q. Was it totally unrelated to the BluBlockers?

A. In essence it was totally unrelated. However, if it wasn't for BluBlockers, I would have never been able to do it.

Q. Because of the financing or because people wouldn't have identified you with sunglasses?

A. The relationship was in two areas. One was the fact that we were in the sunglass business. We had found out that there was a movie coming out called "Back to the Future II." The picture takes place in the future when the ozone layer has practically disappeared, and people must wear sunglasses and the sunglasses were very unusual. Since we were pioneering eye protection, we decided that this would be a great movie to feature BluBlockers in. We contacted the movie people and worked very hard in designing unusual pairs of sunglasses for the movie.

The second reason that we got into this was that we had the contacts in the Far East to make the sunglasses. As we developed the various models for the movie and we also created the signage which was to be used in the movie, we found out that Pizza Hut was one of the companies that would be involved. We approached Pizza Hut, with permission from the producers of the movie, to make a presentation and possibly develop a continuity program for sunglasses. In other words, we wanted to offer a different pair of sunglasses each week. We then took all of the models that we created for the movie, presented them to Pizza Hut, and they picked out a couple of them that they really liked.

We then went back to the drawing board to design two more. In the meantime they went through their due diligence and their research and determined: 1) Our designs were better than anything else they could get and, 2) The public really loved our designs and were really excited about the promotion. The public was willing to pay whatever the sunglasses were worth in order to buy them along with the pizza. I had already been a customer of several factories in the Far East. But we needed ten million pair produced in a very short period of time. There was no room for error. The deal we had with Pizza Hut was that if we were not able to supply them the ten million by the deadline, we would not be paid.

We organized a massive production schedule that was to last a month and a half. It was to involve ten or twelve factories. It was the biggest sunglass order in the history of the sunglass business. We completed the order on time. And on budget. The program was a big success. Pizza Hut's average sales increased as a result of the promotion, and the product was sold in New Zealand, Australia, England and in Canada as well as the United States. We had to handle shipments to all those countries.

It was a wonderful experience. It was a great adventure for me. I took ten trips within one year to the Far East. There were some stretches when I lived in the Far East for a month to five weeks. We had a person there constantly. We had representatives of our company consistently going in and out of Taiwan making sure things were being coordinated. We had a big staff here coordinating everything. It wasn't an easy job, because Pizza Hut is a restaurant and every product that came off the production line had to be correct from a sanitation standpoint, clean and packaged properly to protect the sunglasses. Then they had to be inspected very thoroughly with many tests to make sure that they weren't toxic and that they wouldn't harm any child. There were certain times when entire shipments were rejected. It was not an easy program, but we did it and we did it quite successfully.

Q. Murray said he was visiting you one day and you had an entire shipment rejected because you had a problem with the pin mechanism?

A. It was at the very beginning phase of the program. Murray was visiting with me and I had just gotten the news that one of our major suppliers had used a pin that was a little too sharp in the hinge. They had produced a quarter of a million of them with that sharp pin. We had to go back and rework every one of those until they were all correct, but we did it.

Q. How do your failures prepare you for success?

A. It is the lessons that you learn. You rarely learn anything from your success. If everything goes well, you say to yourself, "Boy am I smart. I did everything right." It could be by chance that things worked out correctly. If things don't work out it could also be by chance, but more than likely it is because you did something wrong. You will learn from what you have done wrong.

The important fact is not whether you are successful or whether you fail. The key is whether you've played the game. If you just sit back and don't do anything, you'll never know if you could be successful. If you go out and do something and you're successful, you've won. If you fail you've learned something, and that in itself is an important stride towards success. The more you learn, the sharper you become and the greater the chances that you will become successful.

Q. Reese Palley (see "Sell!" chapter) says that whenever he tried to repeat a success he invariably failed. Do you agree?

A. There is a better way of putting it. There is a point in space and time when things work perfectly. That opportunity is usually presented to you and if you take advantage of it and it does work perfectly, the chances of that space and time being the same some other time in the future are very remote. That is why I always tell people, "Never copy." Because you can copy the concept, you can copy the ideas, you can copy everything else but you can never duplicate that point in time and space.

Q. What do you think of recent media reports that business is bad and that companies are failing?

A. I have a theory about that and that is whenever there are these dramatic changes, there's a tremendous number of opportunities out there as well. It's up to companies to recognize these opportunities. When the economy is bad, I rely more on the basics. In other words, testing is extremely important. I'll be as aggressive as I've always been, but I'll stick to the basics I have learned in marketing. I think that when everybody thinks things are bad, it is a great opportunity because there is something out there that is going to work exceptionally well. You are not going to find it unless you try. If you go out there and test, your losses are going to be small. The potential on the upside is very big and it is worth a shot.

I look at the headlines because I look at how influenced the public must be by certain news headlines. At certain points I use those headlines as opportunities to try new things that take those fears into consideration.

Q. What advice do you give to people who are just starting out in business or are thinking of going it alone after being in a company?

A. I think first of all you have to have the spirit, the drive, the philosophy and the incentive to go off on your own. When someone makes a commitment to go off on their own, they should not give up until they have achieved success.

Q. Did you ever lose your drive and ambition and spirit because of financial problems?

A. There were times when the financial problems were so overbearing that I wondered how I could continue, but I always knew that I would pull myself out. I think it is important for an entrepreneur to know that he or she can make a lot of money and build a nice company and lose it and be able to build it again. I guess probably in the back of my mind I always had that belief that I can do it again, I can do it on a different level or in a different way.

Q. Were you ever tempted to work for a larger company or be a part of a larger business?

A. When I was starting out in business, that was one of the things that I did indirectly because I had my own ad agency, which was in essence like having ten to twelve bosses. It was at that point I realized I couldn't work for somebody. I had to have my own little business. There were a few times when other business were interested in acquiring our company. I resisted primarily because I could not see myself working for somebody else. I just needed my freedom.

There are some people who are just not corporate people, just as there are some people in the corporate world who are not entrepreneurs. It is just a mentality, a mind set.

Q. Do you think your move away from electronics had something to do with there not being as many opportunities to sell electronic products by mail as there were ten years ago?

A. The business that I was in ten to twenty years ago was the introduction of new advanced space-age type products. There was a tremendous amount of excitement every time one of these new products came out. You had to have one.

Q. You helped create the business.

A. The product had to be right. The right product at a certain point in space and time. Consumer electronics was really taking off. It was having it's most rapid growth. It was the beginning of the integrated circuit in its application to many new products. In the early eighties that excitement started to fade. Electronics became a mature industry.

Q. Was the excitement of the BluBlocker sunglasses akin to when you first introduced the electronic calculators as your first products?

A. I think any time you discover a product that the public relates to is a very exciting period of time.

The public helps me discover which products are the winners. I come up with my opinion and say, "Well, based on my opinion, I think this product will be good" and I advertise it. Then I sit back. Not only will the public tell you if its the right product, it will tell you if it is the right advertising medium.

In the case of the BluBlockers, that was a very dramatic example of first of all discovering the product and the public telling me that it was a great product. Then going from a one percent share of the market to the current state of affairs where all of the sunglasses in the market now block UV light.

Q. Stew Leonard (See "Wow!" chapter) tries to sell high quality products at the very minimal price he can make a profit. Is there a difference selling milk at the retail level and selling calculators or sunglasses through the mail?

A. Stew has a very appropriate approach for his business. I know he swears by it. I agree with him that when you're in as competitive a business as he is that price is extremely important and, of course, service is very important. He provides both and does it very effectively and he is a master at what he does. In my business it is a little different. People are willing to pay any price for a product that they feel has perceived value and provides emotional satisfaction and the results that they're looking to achieve with that product.

It is up to us as marketers in direct marketing to realize that we don't have the competition that a grocery might have. We are unique little islands within ourselves and we have to create our own little niche in the market place and offer our products at value. The consumer is very smart. They will tell you whether or not your product is priced right, whether it really fills a need and whether your delivery is appropriate. If it is not, they are going to tell you and nobody is going to tell you otherwise.

Q. So you may have to charge higher prices to make up for all failures that are an inevitable part of your business?

A. No. Not at all. One success has nothing to do with any other failure. They are all separate individual approaches. I can't charge more for a product to make up for something that didn't work.

Q. So it is based on the perceived value and use of the consumer not on how much it costs you to get the product?

A. Correct. There is a point when it is no longer very practical to continue to offer a product if you have to price it low enough so that you lose money. By the same token we run products that have maybe a 10 percent margin and have made a very handsome profit. There are other times when we have had margins of triple the cost of a product and have lost money. Margins have absolutely nothing to do with it. It is perceived value. It is the need you have created. It is the exclusivity of the product you are offering. It is the ease in which those people can obtain that product. It is a point in time and space. At that point in time and space you have to have a lot of your ducks in a row.

Once you get started in that point you develop a momentum. That momentum continues as long as you service your customers properly and as long as you provide a very good product, and as long as you keep yourself focused on those reasons why you were successful to start with. If you do all of that, you will continue to pull ahead of any competitors that come into the field.

Q. As we go in to the nineties are you looking for new areas where you can achieve the right time and place with consumers?

A. No, I don't go out and try to find. I go out and I test.

In the '90s I am very much tuned in to the consumer. I let them tell me everything that is happening in the market place. I do that by sticking my nose out occasionally with either products or promotions, and customers tell me very dramatically and very quickly whether the product will succeed. I am not going to go out there and force a product or concept on the marketplace. The marketplace is going to drag it out of me, and I am going to know how to respond to that marketplace.

SELL!

SELL! INTRODUCTION

After you listen to your customers, you can begin to sell to them. **Because every time two people meet, there is a potential sale.**

There are a lot of different ways to think about the interaction between buyer and seller. Reese Palley (see the interview this chapter) sees it as a wary dance between two somewhat antagonistic forces. Stew Leonard (interviewed in the "Wow!" chapter) views the relationship as the seller trying to provide the best possible product to the buyer at the lowest possible price. And Joe Sugarman (see "Listen!" chapter) thinks the most important facet of the buyer-seller relationship is the "perceived value" of the goods or service.

But whatever focus you put on the relationship between buyer and seller, that interaction remains the epitome of business practice, the method by which good firms prosper and mediocre firms fall to the wayside.

This chapter focuses on what you can do to improve your chances of making the sale — the techniques of making sure buyers buy what you have to sell.

SELL! QUOTES

Eddy Boas (president, I.M.S. Direct Marketing Division, a subsidiary of Dun & Bradstreet) on how to succeed in sales — "Make enough calls. Cold calls are the only way you can learn to become a good salesman. You have to get your knocks before you can appreciate what success is all about."

Joe Sugarman on how much margin is needed in selling a product — "We have run products that have a 10 percent margin and have made a very handsome profit. There are other times when we have had margins of triple the cost of the product and have lost money. Margins have absolutely nothing to do with success. What is important is perceived value and the effectiveness of your advertising message. It is the need you have created, the exclusivity of the product you are offering and the ease in which people can obtain the product."

MURRAY ON SELLING

There's an family joke that goes like this:

A woman walking down the street meets a new mother pushing a baby carriage with infant twins and asks her, "What are their names?"

The mother says, "The one on the left is John the lawyer and the one on the right is Bill the doctor."

My mother didn't relate to that joke.

She knew I would be a salesman from the day I was born. She told that to the reporter who wrote a story in the Troy, New York Record on January 28, 1928, that was headlined:

BOY BORN RECENTLY AT TROY IS 152ND MEMBER OF FAMILY

"Born — a son, Murray Stanley Raphel to Mr. and Mrs. Harry Raphel, 274 Tenth Street.

This is a notice that greeted the public eye in the newspaper on Sunday, January 28 but it did not tell the whole story.

To begin with, Murray is the 152nd and latest member of one of the largest families in this part of the country. A family reunion shortly after his birth resembled a convention and heaped at his cradle was a ton of gifts that will carry lasting memories of the big occasion for some years to come . . ."

The story went on to list the 152 members of my family and ended with, *"They have great plans for Murray's future. As a matter of fact, they have set their minds on this point. No doctor or lawyer for them. Murray is destined to be a successful business man and in the words of his fond parents, "Why shouldn't he be, even if he didn't do business with anyone but his relatives?'"*

I never did much selling to the relatives but I certainly loved selling.

I began delivering groceries at 14 years old and suggested merchandise the customers could buy next time I came around.

I lied about my age and got a job at 16 selling shoes in a chain shoe store on Saturdays.

I continued to sell shoes through high school, earning money to go to college. In college I found a shoe store that hired me for their Wednesday night opening and all day Saturday for $21, which paid for my meals for the week. I didn't see any football games, but I ate pretty well. And I was the first double major in journalism and drama to graduate from Syracuse University.

After college I worked as a traveling manager for Miles' Shoe Stores as they opened new stores in upstate New York.

All the time I was receiving an education not available from reading books or listening to lectures. I was storing up a vast amount of knowledge of why-people-bought-what-they-bought. And when. And how.

When I arrived with wife Ruth in Atlantic City, New Jersey, I thought I would continue selling shoes. But Ruth's sister and her husband had opened a little children's store. They were doing $15,000 a year. (And I tell everyone that we joined them and within 12 months because of my superior knowledge in selling and my creative abilities, we were able, within just one year, to increase the business from $15,000 a year to $16,000 a year!)

This was a different kind of selling.

The chain shoe store selling philosophy was everyone **must** be sold. If I couldn't sell them, the assistant manager would try. If he could not sell them, the manager was called in. The theme was: once seated, once sold. Who cared whether the customer returned or not? The stores were in high traffic areas and there was always another customer.

Contrast this with the little children's shop we now had. **Every** customer was important. **Every** sale was important. **Every** customer **had** to return. We would sit around the dinner table at night and dissect sales.

"Well, the first thing I did is say 'Hello!' when they came in."

"And what did **they** say?"

"And after they bought the snowsuit, we suggested a knit hat. And showed them several colors and styles to pick from."

We quickly learned that giving a customer a choice between something and something is far more powerful that giving them a choice between something and nothing. The question always was: "Which do you like?" **not** "Do you like this?" Because if the customer says, "No," what do you do then?

And slowly, gradually, step-by-step I learned a **new** selling. A taking-care-of-the-customer selling. A show-the-customer-you're-interested- in-**her** selling. Most of all, I gradually learned there is a "rhythm" to selling.

What's that mean?

This: When a customer would come into the store I would immediately become a **different** person. I felt I was walking on stage. It was like going into a bull ring. I suited up, walked into the arena, prepared to do battle. Instead of my weapons being a sword and a cape, they were knowledge of stock and knowledge of the customer. What did they say? How did they say it?

I found myself watching for small signs: A glance towards somewhere else in the store other than at the merchandise I was showing. An indifferent attitude towards me, the clothing, the store.

I quickly learned that selling was **involvement.** Here we were on stage together. I was talking to them and they had to talk back to me. But they didn't know the lines! They had to be cued like a prompter yelling out the words from behind the curtain.

An easy way to do this was to find out something about them: their business, their vacation plans, their home town. **Anything** that could start a conversation on what was interesting to **them.**

Once that line of conversation opens, the selling changed from the dominant part to a **part** of the dialogue.

And yes, there was a rhythm that made selling work. It's a difficult, almost indescribable concept to explain. But when it's there, it's there. You and the customer are riding along together and enjoying the mood, the moment, the special time and place. If the phone rings for you, if someone calls your name, you simply do not hear the phone or your name. That's absolutely true. You are someplace else instead.

And if someone comes over to talk to you, to break that rhythm and you stop — well, it's back to the beginning again. It's the director off stage saying, "Please pick up that scene from line 12, page 44." And you have to start all over again . . .

Here's what selling is to me: An exciting, enjoyable, exhilarating experience. And when the sale is made . . . ! Ahhh, there is no greater thrill. There is no narcotic made, no alcoholic beverage brewed, no moment in time as great as having **made the sale!** And it is not the making of the money that makes you feel like this. It is the making of the **sale.** The facing the challenge and winning.

This of course does not mean the customer has lost. On the contrary, the customer has **also** won. But won because you have showed the way, the direction, the reasonss to buy. You have started (or continued) a trusting relationship.

Here's what I discovered very early: People **want** to buy. All you have to do is give them a reason.

Selling is the most personal of professions because there is so much of yourself involved. You pull out all the talents, abilities, know-how you have accumulated through the hundreds or thousands of experiences you have gone through personally.

There will always be that small shot of adrenaline when first walking into the room of the prospective buyer or meeting them on the selling floor. It is the same as the actor going on stage, the speaker walking to the podium. The concealed nervousness, the fear of "Will it work **this** time?"

It was prophetic that mom and dad knew I was going to be a salesman. But I had to go beyond the relatives, beyond the friends, the seemingly never ending line of strangers that appeared before me throughout my life challenging, demanding, making me wonder if I had learned all that had to be learned. Would I know how to overcome objections and turn them into sales? Had I learned all there was to learn about the product I was offering?

And then the distant, mysterious voice inside says, "You're on!" And I walk onto the stage one more time . . .

A GOOD SALESMAN BELIEVES IN HIS PRODUCT

There is a classic story of a man watching other men lay brick.
"What are you doing?" he asked the workmen.
The first one said, "Laying brick."
The second one said, "Making $15 an hour."
The third one said, "Building a cathedral."

A GOOD SALESMAN GIVES A LITTLE EXTRA

When Eddie Cantor was growing up on the lower East Side of
New York City he ran errands for housewives in his tenement
building. In exchange for a piece of cake or a chunk of salami, he
did their grocery shopping.

One thing puzzled him. Why did all the housewives send him to
one store which was ten blocks away. Why not a closer market?
He offered to change, but the housewives all said "No."

The next time he went, he watched carefully to see the reason.
What he **did** see were **mistakes.** If an order was for a dozen rolls,
this grocer put in thirteen. The milk jug was always filled **above**
the quart line. Half a dozen bananas were ordered and charged
for —but the grocer put in seven.

Cantor went to the grocer and pointed out the mistakes he
made. "They're not mistakes, " he said. "It's good business to give
something 'extra'."

Years later, Cantor went back to see if he could find out if the
grocer was still in business. The store was gone but he finally did
locate the grocer. He was now on the upper East Side. He no
longer worked in a store. He was chairman of the board of a chain
of supermarkets.

A GOOD SALESMAN NEVER GIVES UP

I was a junior in high school working in a chain shoe store. It
was one of those days. Nothing worked. Customers left without
buying. Finally the manager yelled at me, "Can't you do anything
right?"

I went to the back of the store, behind a partition. I was sad,
wanting to be somewhere, anywhere else. I didn't have to take

this. I'd find another job. The manager came, saw me upset and yelled, "What are you doing here, Raphel?"

I mumbled something about I couldn't stand him yelling at me and said, "I quit."

"You quit?" he said, "**You quit? You can't quit. You can only quit this job if I say you can quit. And I haven't given you permission to quit.**" And he walked away.

I stayed. And went back to selling. Made a few sales and learned a lesson: Why give up on myself when other people haven't given up on me? After all, I **did** like selling. It was the **not** selling that made me upset.

Pat Knowles, one of the top oil and gas tax shelter sales experts in the nation says, "Every day, my prospects and customers beat me and scratch me and kick me and claw me. But I persist. I help them solve their tax problems and I walk away with big commissions."

A GOOD SALESMAN KEEPS IN TOUCH

I've had three insurance salesmen in my lifetime.

Each approached me the same way asking to do an "audit" of the insurance I had "with no obligation."

Each did an excellent job and took me away from the insurance agent I had because their product was superior or offered more benefits.

And each never saw me again after this sale!

Oh, I **do** receive a birthday card from my present salesman. With his name *stamped* on the card.

But that's it.

Amazing.

And sales people wonder why they are not doing business?

So many times it's because they are so concerned with getting **new** business they forget about the customer they have.

A GOOD SALESMAN SELLS HIMSELF

In an earlier book, "The Great Brain Robbery," written with Ray Considine, we talked about Secret Selling Sentences and said one of them was, "You got me." When selling is fiercely competitive, the strongest selling point sales people can offer is . . . themselves. They are the ones that will be around, available and ready to handle any problem. All things being equal, I'll take the salesman with the commitment to take care of me. *Correction.* I'll pay **more** for the sales person with the commitment to take care of me.

Example: One of the country's top salesmen is Stan Smith of Del Amo Dodge in Torrance, California. Most car salesman make about $25,000 a year. Stan makes close to $200,000 a year selling Dodge automobiles.

No Porsches, Jaguars, BMWs — Dodge cars!

Almost all his customers are repeat customers and referral customers. His secret is that he doesn't sell cars — *he sells himself.*

A customer calls with a newly bought Dodge. The carburetor was dead. The dealer had no replacements in stock. What made it worse: the customer's car is a shuttle service for invalids to and from the hospital.

Stan goes to the showroom floor, takes a carburetor out of new model car and delivers the carburetor to the customer.

PS: Since then the customer has bought 63 Dodge vans from Stan!

Yes, these **are** tough selling times for automobile salesmen. But not for salespeople like Stan Smith.

A GOOD SALESMAN NEVER ACCEPTS SECOND BEST

Sam Solomon was a manufacturer of fine quality children's coats. One day I was in his showroom in New York looking for some extra coats to take back to Atlantic City since our inventory was low. I was in the back room looking over his stock when I overheard a conversation between Sam Solomon and his chief cutter. Solomon was holding up a coat and showing how the herringbone lines did not match on the side seams. He criticized the foreman and said the finished product was unacceptable. Said the foreman, "But we followed the same pattern you made for the solid color coats."

"But this is a herringbone pattern. The lines have to match. Rip out all these coats and sew them all over again."

"But Mr. Solomon," he said, "there's only a few store owners that will see it doesn't match. They'll never know."

" But I know," said Solomon. "And the coats have my name on them."

I waited till they left and quietly walked back to the showroom and doubled the order I was going to buy. Until the day his business closed, he was our primary source for children's coats. I knew that selling would rarely be "tough" for the man who set such high standards because "It has my name on it."

We decided to have the same commitment to quality in our store. If our bag or box held the merchandise, it was **our** product. No matter **what** the label said. The customer always had to be satisfied and always had to expect the best. After all, "It has our name on it."

TEN CHARACTERISTICS OF TOP SALESPEOPLE
(Note: Many of these characteristics were described in Edwin Hoyt's classic book, "America's Supersalesmen.")

1. Work Hard. Promoter Bill Veeck (You remember Veeck. He sent the midget to the plate!) said of his successful baseball franchises in St. Louis, Cleveland and Chicago, "I've met a lot of people that are smarter than I am, but I never met anyone that worked harder." And be happy in your hard work. There is an old Chinese proverb, "He who cannot smile should not own a shop."

2. Be self-confident. Your customers will believe in you if you believe in yourself. Dodge salesman Stan Smith (mentioned earlier this chapter) tell his customers not to worry about anything going wrong in their cars. "You buy me!" Stan says. And his customers know Stan will take care of any problems with their cars.

3. Have self-discipline. Alan Laiken in his book "How to Get Control of Your Time and Life," tells people to divide all their mail into three piles: "A" (the most important), "B" (the not-so-important) and "C" (the least important). Then throw the C pile away. Take the B pile, divide it into an A and C pile, and again throw the C pile away. Take the A pile, divide it into 1-2-3 priorities and tackle the #1 priorities first. That's self-discipline.

4. Have perseverance. A salesman used to call on us with merchandise we felt not right for our store. After a few seasons we asked him how long he was going to call since we consistently turned down his line. "Well," he said, "It depends on which one of us dies first . . ." A McGraw-Hill survey said on average it takes five repeat calls for a salesman to get that first order from a client.

5. Be flexible. If you send out a mailing piece to a test market and the response is low, change the copy. Or the mailing list. Or the product. It is fine to live on high expectations. But if the realities tell you otherwise, you must be flexible.

6. Have goals other than money. Millionaires were interviewed by Merv Griffin and he asked them if money was a driving force in their lives.

Each said no. One said there was the challenge to make a jet plane for individuals instead of just for airline companies. Another spoke of perfecting a food recipe and selling it to the mass market. Each in turn said they "had this idea," believed in it and worked for it.

Famed newscaster Bernard Meltzer tells of the time he was trying to raise money to go to college. Though accepted by tuition-free CCNY in New York City, he needed $100 for books. He approached a friend of the family he called Uncle Joe. He told him of the problem. Uncle Joe handed him a check for $100. Meltzer, overwhelme, said, "I don't know when I can pay you back the money . . ."

Uncle Joe replied, "You can never give me back the money, Bernard. I will not accept it. However, there will come a time in the future when you will be successful. And someone will come to you for help. You must leave your door open and you must listen, and you must try to be of assistance. And then you can say, 'I'm paying back Uncle Joe . . .'"

7. Have respect for the buyer's good sense. The con man making a living from hit-and-run will not obtain true success. His triumphs are of the moment, his success illusory. Only when you know and understand the problem of the customer will you develop the answer to his or her needs.

We once went with a local real estate consultant to a bank officer for a real estate loan. Our meeting lasted less than five minutes and we received immediate approval.

"What happened?" we asked in the hallway after the meeting. "Why did he say yes so quickly?"

The learned, older real real estate man looked at us and slowly said, "I never ask a question unless I know the answer is yes."

Our real estate consultant had assembled all the critical and necessary information. He summarized it quickly and presented the total package within a few minutes. The loan officer found all the necessary documentation he needed without having to give long explanations and detailed questioning. He gave his approval.

Our consultant simply knew what the customer wanted. . . and gave it to him. And the sale was made.

8. Be willing to learn from others. My father used to sell insurance for Metropolitan Life Insurance Company. It was the time of the depression. He collected a quarter a week premium from customers. One day he told a customer, "Instead of coming to the door every week, simply leave the quarter in an envelope with your receipt book in your mailbox."

She agreed. He did this for six months. One week he opened the mailbox and saw his envelope with the quarter. And another envelope from the Prudential Insurance Company with another quarter.

He rang the bell. The customer answered the door. "Tell me," he said. "Are you mad at me?"

"Why no," she said. "Why would you think so?"

He explained he collected her premium every week for six months. Today he saw another insurance policy — written by his competition.

The woman looked surprised and said, "Oh. Do you sell insurance. I thought you were just a collector."

From that moment on, my father always told his customers he was a life insurance **salesman**.

9. Be able to handle big money. People who handle big money use it as a tool the way a carpenter uses his tools or a chemist uses his tools.

An experienced clothing buyer said, "I know my budget. I am conscious of units. But if I start relating my 'buying dollars' to the dollars in my pocketbook, I would run screaming from the room."

10. Be a perfectionist. Former President Jimmy Carter tells of the time he was a captain in the Navy and reported to his superior, Admiral Rickover, after completing an assigned task.

"I have completed the job," said Carter.

Rickover looked up from his desk and quietly said, "Is it the very best you could do?"

"Pardon, sir?" said Carter not quite sure what the Admiral meant.

"Did you do the very best you could possibly do on that job?" said Rickover.

Carter hesitated and then said, "I'll check it out sir, and report back."

Carter doublechecked and triplechecked his work. He came back and said, "Sir, it's the best job I could possibly do."

Rickover did not look up from his desk. "Dismissed," he said. He knew Carter would not come back until the job was perfect.

Good salespeople appreciate the attitude of Admiral Rickover. They are not satisfied until they do the very best they can do.

INTRODUCTION TO REESE PALLEY INTERVIEW

Reese Palley is a 21st Century visionary with the soul of a 19th Century peddler.

We do not endorse all of Reese Palley's thoughts, ideas and suggestions about selling. But some of his "off-the-wall" dictums have more than a small dash of wisdom.

One of the best salesmen we have ever encountered, Reese operated an art gallery for years in Atlantic City. He achieved a certain notoriety by being the self-proclaimed "Merchant to the Rich." When Atlantic City turned to gambling, so did Reese. He bought an option on a fancy old decaying Atlantic City resort hotel, and with typical panache sweet talked his way to a multimillion dollar profit by selling the property to a casino.

Reese is a born salesman ("Give me a pushcart and some costume jewelry and I'll do very well"). But now he is taking techniques of selling honed over an active two score and ten years of existence and using them to break new ground.

His sailing retirement has been interrupted by political and economic events in Russia and Romania. With his uncanny knack for being where the action is, Reese sailed into Odessa, Russia the day in 1988 Gorbachov declared, "All power to the people." Figuring that he was in a great position to show the Eastern Europeans a thing or two about capitalism, Reese quickly formed trading companies that did business with Russians and Romanians.

Today, Reese is finding new ways to peddle Marlboro cigarettes to Romanians and IBM mainframes to Russians. Other partners near Odessa are farming mushrooms and associates in Romania are planning a marina complex.

When he describes his various adventures and projects, one gets the impression that they all fall into one grand scheme of exporting capitalism to those who need it most.

Or maybe it's just that Reese has sold us a bill of goods.

Put a padlock on your wallet!

Reese Palley has arrived.

Let the selling begin!

REESE PALLEY INTERVIEW

Q. How do you sell a product?

A. If it won't sell, raise the price. There's always a price where something will sell. The other tip is never sell an object. Always sell excitement, the sizzle rather than the steak.

It's gonna be a helluvalot easier for good peddlers to operate in the 1990s than it was in the 80s because in the 1980s we were cluttered up with too much demand and too many second rate people were out there confusing the market. In the 90s you're not going to have all of that loose money around to promote stuff by just the pressure of the advertising. You're gonna have to be smart. It's the smart guys that are going to do it. It's gonna be a cleaner marketplace and be easier for good people who have creative ideas to go ahead and get their message across.

Q. Someone once asked you how to get rich and you said, "Don't pay your bills!" But isn't it true that a good selling relationship is based upon trust?

A. That was one of the quotes I used to say to "brick the camel," to get attention. But there is a kind of truth in it. You obviously have to pay your bills. But you don't have to pay **all** of your bills. If you're a poor guy and you don't have any debt you can always generate some credit, but those are the bills you never pay because you keep buying. If you continue to do business with a firm they will capitalize you. If you do business with 100 firms, your whole business can be capitalized by those firms. It's a simple matter. It doesn't have anything to do with the morality of owing money or not owing money. I am not wildly worried about the morality problem.

Q. Do you agree with the statement that good long term business relationships have to be based on trust?

A. Between whom?

Q. Between the person selling the product and the person buying it.

A. It's kind of a trust built on an antagonistic position. There's no contract going to be made unless there's some level of trust. But the buyer is convinced he is getting screwed, and the seller is convinced he has an advantage. So it is not the kind of trust you get in a non-commercial relationship. It is a trust that says there is an acceptable amount of swindling going on both sides, but that's the price we have to pay for making a contract.

Q. I thought all good economic transactions must be mutually beneficial?

A. That's exactly what I said.

Q. Are you saying that even though they are mutually beneficial there is a little bit of swindle going on?

A. There is a knowledge, a perception on both sides that the other guy is always taking a little advantage. You don't always get the best deal. You get the deal you can get. There is always a sense that I can get a little better the next time. Trust is a WASP concept. When families have been doing business together for 100 years and they have been swindling other people, there's trust between them. A gentlemen's agreement. People who have this kind of trust write each other checks and they call each other up and they do their deals. The trust is based on the advantage that this old money has over new money. So it's kind of a selective trust.

Q. Let's take your situation. You've been selling all your life and now you're starting to sell to Eastern Europeans. Why?

A. It has to do with the grip that a little guy can get on fundamental processes.

Q. But you've always been 20 years ahead of everybody else. Do you think that in the 90s more and more people are going to be turning to Eastern Europe?

A. You've heard the expression, "The early bird gets the worm." I have discovered that more likely the early bird gets eaten by a hungry cat. So it's not always a good idea to be ahead except in your own mind. It is delicious to look back and say, "I was 20 years ahead." Incidentally, that time scale is shortening. You don't have to be 20 years ahead. You can be 20 minutes ahead in America and in Eastern Europe all you have to be is six months ahead.

I think it's very clear that success for the good peddlers is going to be based on the profound understanding of communication. Selling is not going to decline. You're going to be out there selling to people you don't understand, you don't really know, or it may take too long to find out about. I think demographics has very little relevance to selling in Eastern Europe in the 90s.

Demographics is a concept which is used to define small advantages within a market which has a tremendous amount of opportunity. But, in Romania I can't get demographics at all. They are all lies. It's like the maps of Moscow. You know that maps of Moscow are all wrong. They point you in the wrong direction so in case the Americans invaded, they wouldn't know where to go. So it is not going to be a so carefully engineered sales force.

Q. You talk about being a peddler in the 90s and yet for years you were self-described as a "Merchant for the Rich." Is there a difference between merchant and peddler?

A. There is absolutely no difference. Give me $100 worth of costume jewelry and a cart and I can make a living anywhere. I think of myself as a peddler. The ancient term for merchant is someone who walks around and sells things so that the peddler term is honest.

Purveyor to the rich is bullshit. Or what's even more bullshit is purveyor to the well-to-do. That would upset nobody. "Merchant to the rich" — rich is a four letter word. "Merchant to the rich" upset many more people than it pleased. They thought it was an arrogant statement. Tear the statement apart and it is nothing. It says I'm selling things to rich people. There is a perception of arrogance about that kind of statement.

Q. You've been involved in the art world. You've sold a hotel to a casino. You're now working in Russia. You must like moving on to the next challenge.

A. You move along and get out and get it out of your hair. I've known a lot of people who have a great idea and instead of realizing that ideas are cheap and moving on to the next thing, they hold on to an idea for their whole life. They have that one idea over and over and over and it goes out of date.

I once knew a brilliant young architect who designed an invalid's chair, a self-rising chair. He designed it, won a prize for it and for the next twenty years he used up his professional life on that chair. So it's not a question of brilliance for a great salesman. It's a matter of being able to release an idea and not live with it. Do it. Move on. Because ideas change.

Q. Don't repeat. Do the next thing.

A. You may repeat on a different level. The idea is to give up the successful. If it's successful, forget about it. I'll give you an example. I did a trip to Paris. It's a fairly famous thing where I rented a couple of 747's.

Q. I have the original invitation.

A. I took 750 of my favorite personal friends and we did it. We made a lot of money and a lot of publicity. It was a sensation. And I didn't follow my own instincts. Because the next year we did the same trip to Italy and we made money on it. But it was half the size and half the excitement. And then we did one to Africa. And then one to Israel and that never went through. The point is that we wasted our lives for three years trying to repeat an initial success which was an accident. You can have a great idea. But the real big ones feed on input that you never anticipate.

Q. *So the moral of that story would be that once you have a great success, it can be time to move on?*

A. Bury it. Bury it. It is the time to move on. You are going to use up energy trying to repeat that success and you can't do it.

Q. *You talk about believing in the things that you are selling. Did you really believe in the Boehm birds and the Dali prints and the other things you sold in your store?*

A. No, of course not. Belief has nothing to do with taste. Please, you are confusing the issue. I believed in the process. I believed in my customers. I believed in the fun and excitement I could build around these birds. I believed in the other things that we sold. We sold a great many things that I not only believed in, but I believed in the good taste of.

Q. *What did you believe in about the birds that made you able to sell them? Did you believe that the customers enjoyed them?*

A. Yes. The birds added a dimension of excitement to the lives of my customers. I was extending the horizons of their lives. I was bringing them into an exclusive club where they were able to have a sense of mixing with events larger than themselves.

Who were they? They were rich, aesthetically deprived Jews, who had recently made a lot of money. And I say that with love. I don't say that with anger. It is better to have been nouveau riche than never riche at all.

Here's a story. A little fat guy and his wife walked into my shop one day and she was wearing the cocktail rings, the dumpy suit and he had his belt down under his belly and his cigar was dripping ashes. The wife looks around and finally settles on a very expensive pattern of china. So my salesperson comes to me and says, "Hey, Reese you better talk to them because she's picked out something that's going to cost $1000." So I came over and took the guy aside and said, "Look, I don't want to embarrass you. But I want you to know, my friend, that your wife has picked out a pattern of china that is going to cost her $1000 and I want you to be aware of that." And he takes his cigar out of his mouth and leans back and flicks the ashes down onto his big belly and says, "Think nothing of it. We're nouveau riche."

Q. *You started out in Atlantic City? What are the Atlantic City casinos doing wrong? Some are losing money. Some are going out of business.*

A. They are selling a product. They are not selling excitement. They should be selling excitement. Vegas is selling excitement.

Q. *Is there a difference between a Las Vegas casino and an Atlantic City casino?*

A. Sure there is. It is the sweet smell of sin. We don't have that yet. You have to have that sweet sense of something beyond your normal life. Winning or losing is not the only reason for the success of casinos. The casinos that were associated with the mafia in Vegas were always more successful than the others. People liked to be involved with the demi world.

In New Jersey there is no demi world. We've eliminated all the interesting people in the casinos.

Q. *Donald Trump wanted to be bigger and better and built the Taj Mahal. He tried to make it exciting. Where did he go wrong?*

A. He didn't try to make it exciting. He tried to build exciting structures. He was constrained within the same limits that Bally, Caesars and the rest of them are in Atlantic City.

Q. *So it's the rules?*

A. It's the rules . . . it's the law. The pattern in which gambling was granted was infinitely middle class.

Q. *So the casinos don't have the flexibility with the gaming to make it work?*

A. The gaming, the whores, the girls, the shows, you have to have a kindle. You know, casino is sex and if you don't have the perception of immorality in gambling, you can't succeed. Vegas was always able to sell the idea that gambling was immoral — the association of the mafia and all the rest. We managed to construct moral gambling in New Jersey. Nobody is really interested.

Q. *Is Atlantic City doomed?*

A. It's a great tragedy. Because there was a moment where we could have made a sensational city . . . **sinsational** . . . well that's only half of it. The other half of it is Disneyland.

Q. *And there was a chance in the 70s?*

A. When gambling passed, the laws should have said the people who work in Atlantic City cannot live in Atlantic City. My quote was, "Atlantic City needs a bulldozer 10 blocks wide." I still believe it. You need golf courses. You need riding trails. You need Disneyland. You need all the ancillary excitements that we have not put in this town because the law was so stringent about not displacing people and because the casino people themselves were so shortsighted. It just came down to a strip on the Boardwalk and it becomes uglier and uglier.

Q. *What was the hardest thing you ever had to sell?*

A. I once went up to Spode, a china house, and they took me down the basement and showed me 100 cubic meters of pottery. Ugly blue pottery. They sold it to me for a quarter a pound. And I figured I could sell it. I bought all the Spode. I have to tell you it used up a big part of my basement and a big part of time.

I put it out at regular price and I made a sign that said, "Buy our mistakes for half price." Worked like a charm. We paid our rent with that for two years. By admitting it was a mistake. Not saying here's a great bargain. If I had said, buy this ugly horseshit for half price, I'd have sold more.

Q. *Advertising in American isn't very humorous. Should it be more toward bad taste humor?*

A. All we used was humor. One of the greatest ads we ever did was shortly after gambling came in. We took a full page New Yorker ad which showed me with one hand behind my back holding up a Boehm bird, and it said "Atlantic City's original one armed bandit." It worked like a charm. We did that consistently.

Q. *What are the rules for selling that every merchant should know?*

A. Never listen to expert advice. Keep raising the price until you find the price at which a thing will sell. Be funny. Respect the perception of your buyer that you're cheating him. And that's crucial. If you can understand that he's not much dumber than you are, and you respect him and you tell him the truth and you tell him the brutal truth, the chances are he'll listen to you.

WOW!

WOW ! INTRODUCTION

Enthusiasm is contagious.

One person comes into work every day, greets everyone with a smile and a compliment. People smile back and like that person.

Another person comes into work every day, doesn't greet anyone, looks at the floor as he walks around, never smiles, doesn't make eye contact with other people. This lack of enthusiasm is also contagious. Deadly. People do not smile back and do not like that person.

Enthusiasm is also habit forming.

People that feel better, act better. Stimulate positive feelings within yourself and those feelings start bouncing back from the people that work with you every day.

Enthusiasm can help counteract "tough times." When your customers and employees see the joy and vigor with which you greet the world, they will want to be around you and do business with you.

An enthusiastic example is speaker Charlie "Tremendous" Jones (when people ask Charlie how he feels, he roars back, "Tremendous!"). Charlie greets everyone with a giant bear hug and a cheery "I want you to remember how glad I am to see you!"

Now that's the right way to start every day.

WOW ! QUOTES

"Enthusiasm can't be taught. It must be caught." — Dale Carnegie

"A man can succeed at almost anything for which he has unlimited enthusiasm" — Charles Schwab

From our Australian friend Tony Ingleton (see chapter on "Reward!")

"About eight or nine months ago, I had a lot of pressure, financial pressure, in terms of meeting bills, working out the cash flow, etc . . . And it really started to get me down.

"Then I realized that I had a role as leader of my business. That role didn't mean simply that you made the payroll each week. It also meant that you are in charge of the enthusiasm of the company. And if the head person is giving out very bad vibes, that isn't going to do anyone any good.

"So, even if I am literally bleeding inside, when I pick up the phone I sound happy, positive, as if I didn't have a problem in the world. And, immediately, I start to feel better. If I have a happy look on my face, I find that happiness comes through in my voice."

HOW ENTHUSIASM CHANGED SOCCER

It was an important game of soccer between two English schools. They were traditional rivals and the score was tied with just seconds left to play. One team member was a young boy with more enthusiasm than experience. His team had a lot of injuries and the coach sent him in during these last few moments of the game.

He ran onto the field and was so excited he forgot all the rules, including the one that a soccer player does not touch the ball with his hands. All he knew was that he had to get the ball across the goal line within seconds if his team were to win. On the next play he picked up the ball in his arms and ran like a frightened animal across the goal line.

The officials and players looked on in disbelief. But the people in the grandstand became hysterical in the excitement and stood up and cheered the young man.

The memorable day marked the birth of a new national sport that was named Rugby —in honor of the school where it happened. And it all happened because of one young man's enthusiasm!

CUT OUT THE COMPLAINTS

A friend recently told of an experience they had with a doctor's receptionist who was curt, cold and gave them a difficult time.

"Well, then," I said,"the doctor is also curt, cold and will give you a difficult time."

It's true. We tend to imitate what we think is expected of us. Businessman Ross Perot says people don't need to be managed. They need to be led. How you act, react, perform is closely watched by the people all around. They imitate.

Here is an observation I believe in:

"Cut out the complaints and most people have nothing to say."

Listen to the people around you and their conversations.

"Did you see what the (check one: president/ mayor/ governor/ someone) did today? Can you believe that?"

"Isn't the weather terrible! It's too (check one: hot/ cold/ rainy/ foggy)."

"Did you see what's happening in the (check one: Mid East/ Europe/New Jersey)?"

The next time that happens to you, look the person straight in the eyes and quietly ask, "What do you want me to do about that?"

They will look at you strangely and go away. That's fine.

Or, better yet, the next time someone comes to you with complaints, answer this way: "I understand you're upset. I want to help. What I do **not** want to do is become sad and unhappy. So if you want to sit down and figure out how we can solve that problem, terrific. Let's do it together."

Inventor Charles Kettering said, "A problem well stated is half solved."

What began as a negative situation turns into a positive situation because you changed the atmosphere from complaining about the problem to enthusiastically planning to solve the problem.

Once you stop worrying about a problem and start planning a solution, good things start to happen.

WHAT PEOPLE WORRY ABOUT

People generally tend to worry too much about everything. Many people invent something to worry about so they can get through the day with a problem that gives them an excuse for not doing the job, making the sale, creating a happy environment.

This is not only self-defeating it is self-destructive. Doctors have proven that worry cuts down your life span as well as your success span.

Try this one: More Americas commit suicide (the result of stress, anxiety and yes, worry) than die from the five most common communicable diseases.

Worry causes heart trouble, high blood pressure, asthma, rheumatism, colds, arthritis, migraine headaches and a host of stomach disorders in addition to ulcers.

So why are you worried?

A recent survey on "Things People Worry About" broke down as follows:

Things that never happen:	40 percent
Things that can't change:	30 percent
Needless worry about health:	12 percent
Petty and miscellaneous worry:	10 percent
Real problems:	8 percent

Conclusion: 92 percent of the things people worry about, they can't do anything about!

SELLING TICKETS

Sometimes problems seem so huge as to be unmanageable. The solution: Break the problem down to small solvable pieces.

We once did a seminar for the World Hockey Association. One team owner came up to me after the program and said, "I've been listening to you all day and you haven't answered my basic question: 'How do you sell 10,000 tickets?'" We looked at him and quietly said, "One at a time."

It's difficult focusing on 10,000 tickets.

It's easy to focus on **one** ticket.

SPELL YOUR WAY TO SUCCESS

There is a program we do for seminars called Winners and Losers. We tell the audience it is very easy to tell the difference between one and the other because the first letter of each word spells out the characteristic of both **WINNERS** and **LOSERS**. Since one of the key words is Enthusiasm this is a good place to tell you how it works:

W I N N E R S

W stands for Work Hard. We don't know any better way for people to succeed than by simply working hard. They cannot do this unless they enjoy what they are doing. Then the work is no longer "work" in the commonly accepted sense. It is simply something people love to do!

I stands for Ideas. Never tell a Winner there's only one way to do something. "Really?" they'll say and quickly snap off three (or more) ideas you can use to accomplish the same tasks.

N stands for Now. Winners do things **now**! They don't wait for tomorrow, next week or "some other time." They know the desk that is full of work to be done today is twice as full tomorrow if nothing is done. You can always interrupt a Winner during the day and ask for advice and direction and they will **never** say, "See me later." They **will** say, "Try this. If that doesn't work, try this. And if **that** doesn't work, come back again . . ."

N stands for Natural. Watch Winners work. People around them shake their heads and say, "How did they do that?" It is much like watching an outfielder catch the difficult fly ball, the tennis player returning the smashing serve. It looks so easy, so natural, that you feel you could do it as well.

E stands for Enthusiasm. Which is this chapter.

R stands for Repeat. Winners Repeat. If something works, they do it again. Why not? They **will** try to add something new or different to make it work even better. But they will not give up on a wining presentation, idea, or direction until something better comes along.

S stands for Sell. Because that's what Winners do best. And all the time.

L O S E R S

L stands for Later. Losers do **not** do things now. They do them "Later."

O stands for Overworked. "Wait a minute. I was hired to be a salesperson. You mean I also have to fill out reports. And make action plans. And come up with a selling pattern. Hey, I'm overworked!"

S stands for Sorry. "I knew I was supposed to handle that sale and I forgot. I'm sorry." "I'm sorry I didn't have the report ready when you wanted."

E stands for Excuses. "Let me give you the reasons why I wasn't able to get done what you wanted."

R stands for Reject. Every time you come up with a new idea, Losers give you a reason it can't be done.

S stands for . . . nothing. Because Losers Never Finish.

Don't be a Loser. Be a Winner. Everybody loves a Winner. Especially one with . . . Enthusiasm.

AN ENTHUSIASTIC THOUGHT

General Douglas MacArthur had a plaque on the wall of his headquarters when he commanded the Allied Forces in the South Pacific in World War II. (Dale Carnegie had the same quote in his office.) It is from Samuel Ullman, a 19th century rabbi and scholar:

You are young as your faith,
As old as your doubts;
As young as your self-confidence;
As old as your fears;
As young as your hope;
As old as your despair.
Years may wrinkle the skin,
But to give up enthusiasm
Wrinkles the soul.

INTRODUCTION TO STEW LEONARD INTERVIEW
WOW!!!

Let's begin the Stew Leonard story with a healthy dose of enthusiasm! And there's no way of writing about Stew Leonard without a lot of exclamation points!!!!

His supermarket (or dairy store-with-enthusiasm!) does more business per square foot than any other retail establishment in the world! (See Ripley's Believe It Or Not!)

All his four children work in the business. Recently, daughter Jill (head of team member training) came to visit us with a new project. We talked about the project for awhile and in the midst of our conversation Jill suddenly exclaimed, "Wow! What a great idea! This is turning into a great one-idea trip, and that was the one idea! It's made the trip fantastic!"

We felt great. Our idea was good, but Jill's enthusiasm made it great! And all the Leonards are the same way.

We were walking with Stew Leonard's son, Stew Leonard, Jr. ("Stewie"), through their supermarket.

Stewie came upon a group of schoolchildren who were having a school tour through the store. "Now kids," Stewie said, "Raise your hands if you want a glass of water."

None of the kids raised their hands.

"Raise your hands if you want an ice cream cone!" Stewie said.

All the kids raised their hands.

"Ok, ice cream for everyone!" exclaimed Stewie! "Now, are you kids having a good time?"

"Yeah," the kids all said.

"I can't hear you!" said Stewie.

"YEAH!!!!" shouted the kids.

All the Leonards are like good politicians, striving to keep their constituents happy. A huge suggestion box stands in the middle of the supermarket. All suggestions are answered and acted upon by eleven o'clock in the morning.

A giant rock greets you as you enter the supermarket.

Rule #1 is carved into the rock. "The customer is always right."

Rule #2 is carved below. "If the customer is ever wrong, reread rule #1."

And then there is the entertainment. Wow the Cow and Dafney the Duck hug, dance with and tickle the customers. Large mechanical milk cartons croon to the customers. Every so often in one of the 30 checkout lines (30 checkout lines!), you hear a loud "Moo!" Another customer has won a free ice cream cone!

Employees (Oops! Team members!) wear badges with their names in large print and get bonuses if they remember **your** name. The walls are filled with Team Members of the Month and members of the Team Member Hall of Fame. There is "Stew's News" for the team members, which highlights shining examples of customer service.

Stew Leonard, Sr. is now chairman of the board and his children are in charge of day to day affairs of the supermarket. Stew Leonard, Jr. ("Stewie") is president of the company. Son Tom heads their new supermarket in Danbury, Connecticut. Daughter Beth is responsible for all the delicious aromas emanating from the in-store scratch bakery. And daughter Jill is in charge of personnel and training.

It is true that Stew does spend a good portion of the year in St. Martin (connected to Connecticut with fax machines and phones.) But when we went to interview Stew recently in Connecticut it was easy to see his heart was still in the running of the supermarket. He still greets all employees with a big hello or bear hug. He still picks up every stray piece of trash on the supermarket floor. If a food shelf is not piled high enough, or a sale sign does not look quite right, Stew will have someone make the necessary changes. Now!

Stew is still the spokesman for the company (His picture sits on top of the large Suggestion Box). And so when we went to visit Stew, we saw a man relaxed enough to be composing his autobiography, yet passionate enough to get fired up as he answered our questions.

Our assumption was that most businessmen would be a bit wary about opening a new giant supermarket in the midst of a recession. But not Stew. When we implied that times were tough, the sparks began to fly . . .

INTERVIEW WITH STEW LEONARD

Q. Are we now in tough times for retailers? Is now a tough time to go into business or be in business?

A. No. It never is a tough time. If you believe times are tough, times will be tough. You know the old saying about the hammer. You start nailing and say, "I don't want to hit my thumb. I don't want to hit my thumb. I don't want to hit my thumb." Whacko. Owwww! Well, that's what you don't want to do in business.

I saw chicken manufacturer Frank Perdue recently. He said, "Stew, business is really off, isn't it?" I said, "Who said that?"

We just started a gift basket business. We are shipping so many gift baskets out, we can't ship them fast enough. Of course, we are selling a $54.95 basket that everybody else gets $125 for. We're giving tremendous value. People want gift baskets. And people have to eat. Now, people may buy cans of popcorn for $17.95 instead of maybe a $40 or $50 or $60 gift basket. That's true too. But so what. Take a look at our business: Two years ago customers were buying jumbo shrimp at $18.95 a pound. Now they're buying meat and potatoes. In five years if they are going to buy rice, who's going to sell them the rice? I'll sure be trying to.

What is business? As long as people are going to eat and breathe and live, they're going to have to spend money. And as long as they're going to spend money, our job is simply to give them what they want.

As David Ogilvy said, "The customer is not a moron. She's your wife." All you have to do is listen when you get home. What does your wife talk about all the time? She's trying to get a better deal.

Rich or poor, wives like to save money. Everybody basically is looking for a better deal, is looking for better stuff, is looking for an angle, is looking for a coupon, a cut-out, get a free mayonnaise, whatever. Our job is simply to give them what they want. In these "tough times," as you like to call them, we all just have to work a little harder at it.

I don't think we should get credit for being clever just because we put up a suggestion box in the stores and have regular focus groups. That should be a given. A woman wrote me the other day and said, "I have a beautiful brownie recipe. Can I sell it to you?" I said to her, "But the brownie recipe itself isn't the thing that has the big value. I can go down to the library and get 762 brownie recipes. But I can't make them in my own kitchen and sell them. That's what you ought to do." I wrote two pages to this lady. I said, "Why don't you do what Margaret Rudkin did? She started Pepperidge Farms that way. Debbie Fields did it with her cookies."

About two or three months went by, and I received another letter from the woman: "About the meeting I'd like to have with you about my brownie recipe. I have other recipes. And I haven't done anything about it. And I'd love to sit down and we could discuss . . ." What I'm saying is that the problem with many people who start a business is that they are not doing what the original Henry Ford did. Do it. Go make a car. Go bake cookies. Stop talking about it.

Too many people make studies and write plans. What I'm trying to say is the way to do it is to open up the lemonade stand and give the people a better deal. And if people want pink lemonade you add cherry juice and make it pink. You give the customers what they want. You focus on customers. Forget the profit. The profit will come, as long as you generate the volume.

I'm not trying to say it's easy. It's hard. But I am telling you not to listen to the people that tell you times are bad and you should wait ten years and then open your business, when times might be better. Right now is as good a time as ever.

Open the business tomorrow. And start doing it on a small scale. Robert Townsend who wrote "Up the Organization" said, "Start small. Start in your kitchen. If your wife kicks you out, go to the garage. Keep your overhead down. Start small. Stay small. Don't expand. Get out of debt. When you are small and you are out of debt and everyone wants your product, expand with your own profits." But the average person does the opposite.

First they go out and get their MBA. Then they want leverage and partners. I think they're focusing on the wrong thing. Instead they should be figuring out how to give the customer better lemonade at a better price. They're worrying too much about plans and financials. That's why 80 percent of new businesses fail. The key is to ask yourself: "What am I doing? Why am I doing it? Who needs my product? How am I going to serve customers better than others?"

In a nutshell . . . more action is needed and less talk. End of sermon.

Q. Let's go back a bit to when you were first starting out and had a large debt load? How did you keep the enthusiasm up?

A. I guess you mean, "Who motivates the motivator?" That's a good question. Because all of us who run organizations or businesses have to be our own motivator. Around here, we pump each other up. We motivate each other by being enthusiasts.

You just mentioned "employees." Around here we never call people employees. I don't think the people on the firing line like the term. We think it's much better to say "team member." I wouldn't call Wendy who just came in with the coloring book for your daughter an employee. And I think if I did she would get hurt.

If you liken it to a football team, you could say that my job is owner standing on the sidelines and my son Stew, Jr. is the quarterback, and then we have the offense and the defense. And we all have our job to do and we all are aiming to get a Super Bowl ring. Sure the quarterback makes more than the left tackle. But he earns it. We're all one big family. All on the same team — working together to win.

Q. But how do you get yourself motivated every day when you have the pressures of the world on your shoulders?

A. That's easy to answer. I have no pressures of the world on my shoulders. I'm having a ball. Its fun to come to work and create happy customers. With me, personally, our family had a little business that was doing about $230,000 a year when my father died. We had four milk trucks delivering to homes. Suddenly a state highway was planned to be built right through our dairy farm property. At the same time, competitors were opening discount milk stores all around us. My brother Jim and I struggled. We were on our way down the tubes because there was no hope in continuing the home delivery dairy business.

We needed an new idea. I needed some way to save our little business that was going to be wiped out when the highway came. Jim decided to retire to Florida, but I was too young to retire.

So here's what I did. I discovered someone else who was in my business doing a better job than I was. The business was called Gouz Dairy. If I had to look back on my life and name one of the turning points, I'd certainly say this moment was it. I went back to Gouz many times over the next several months. Whenever I would get down in the dumps, I'd go down to Gouz and sit in the parking lot. I would be inspired by the success of the person I hoped to emulate. Obviously, I never dreamed I'd be as big as Gouz someday. Now it's beyond my wildest dreams. I would have been thrilled with a little piece of his business and been a happy guy. I was just a milkman. Gouz inspired me tremendously.

So now we have what we call our "one idea trip." We have a little van and we take people on one idea trips. You go someplace, sometimes it's a friend, sometimes it's a stranger, you call them up ahead of time. Usually they are very happy to have you come.

You go there. You study their business. You get ideas. You don't copy anything. You get inspired. You get pumped up. You get ideas that you can then bring home and use. And we do that constantly. Everytime I go on a vacation, I drag my wife Marianne through a supermarket searching for new ideas and inspiration. I've talked to many other food store owners about it. Most of them also do the same thing. All you need is one idea to make it worthwhile.

Every town in America has that unique enterprise that was a family business and has grown and is filled with good ideas. In Norwalk, in all modesty, I hope it's Stew Leonard's. I hope people say you have to go see Stew Leonard's. They're doing lots of things different. Why, we'll even bring them to a classroom that we call "Stew Leonard's University" and tell them all the good ideas we've discovered.

Q. Do you come to work every day and bring your problems with you or do you put on a happy face?

A. I bought every single motivational tape known to man and I listened to them in the car. I just kept listening to people who would inspire me, from Dale Carnegie to Robert Schuler and Norman Vincent Peale.

In addition I keep books and books and books of quotations and wisdom of the ages. I think you need inspiration on a daily basis. You have to be motivated constantly. Today I read the back page of the new "Forbes" magazine before I read the rest of the magazine.

I guess my own personal philosophy can best be summed up in my own quote: "Don't walk away from negative people. Run." It's of paramount importance to look over your friends and look over your family. And look over the people you "hang around with." Is there somebody in your little circle of friends who is telling you that you can't do stuff, telling you that you are not good enough? Dump them overboard. You don't need them in your life. They are going to wreck you. Because whatever you are going to be in life, you can never do it with negative thinking.

Some kids are told when they are growing up. "You can't do it. Oh, you fool. What makes you think you can do that?" And the child is dumbfounded all the time. But I believe the children who succeed have somebody in their life that encourages them. The key is to surround yourself with people who will make you feel better and make you like yourself better.

Q. You said don't talk about the profit you are making but the good deal you are giving the customer. I know that is your philosophy. Has that always been a part of your business?

A. No. When I had the home delivery milk route, a half gallon of milk used to cost us about 50 cents. And we used to sell it for 69 cents. The idea was to get as many customers at 69 cents as you could, because you would make 19 cents on every half gallon of milk. Every once in a while, a competitor would come along and offer my customer 68 cents. And if they bought six half gallons they would charge them 66 cents each. We would do everything in our power not to drop the price from 69 cents to 65 or 66 cents.

But when I opened the store, I said, "If it cost me 50 cents for a 1/2 gallon of milk in the old dairy, in the new dairy, I'm going to figure out a way to automate everything and make the milk for 40 cents." Which I did. Then I sold it for 50 cents. My profit was only two nickels. But it was 20 percent! I'd rather make 20 nickels than 4 quarters any day.

In the old days, we wanted to make the big profit on a few customers. No more. I realized what was important to me was not profit but how many customers could I get in here. I used to keep in my office, not a chart of my sales, but my customer count. Why is this Tuesday better than last Tuesday? I was constantly focusing on what I could do to get more customers. I believe that focusing on customers is far more important that focusing on profit. You can't have one without the other. And you must have the customers first.

Give me a business that is doing huge volume and making a little profit on each customer. Others can have the business that is making huge markups and has only few customers. Hey. That's hard. And besides, if you lose a few customers you're in trouble.

Q. That's funny because I have heard people say, especially mail order merchants, that the selling price should have no relationship to what it costs to put the product together.

A. The price you should sell something at is the lowest price you can possibly sell it for on high volume and still make money. And if you have any doubt, go buy the New York Times today and open to the business pages and see what's happened to the wholesale clubs in America. And you ask me about profits. They work on eight percent margin. And they are starting to take America by storm.

Several years ago, I took my family down to my friend Sam Walton in Little Rock, Arkansas. It was the grand opening of his first Sam's Wholesale Club. And I came back and I bought some stock. It was the best thing I ever did. I met Sol Price and his son Robert in California. Sol was the originator of the wholesale club idea. So I bought his stock. I believe that the wholesale club is the wave of the future. The customer today is searching to save money. Most wives are working. It's a different world out there. You can't do it the same old way any more. You've got to give your customers a better deal. Go for the 20 nickels!

Q. But how can you give great value when you are providing all the entertainment and the free samples and all the extra amenities?

A. The answer is the magic word "volume." Create volume and you can do lots of extra things. It's so exciting for me. And as you grow bigger, it becomes even more exciting. Then you get your children involved and you keep enthusing them and it's like a snowball coming down the side of a Swiss mountain. But the key word is "volume." With an empty store, there's no money to do anything.

Q. Can you separate your family life and your business life when your kids are working with you on a day to day basis?

A. No problem. But at times it does get a little difficult. At Thanksgiving dinner you sit down and every item on the table came from your family's store. Everybody starts talking about the turkey and how it compares to last year. Every item on the Thanksgiving table except the nut bread that Beth made herself came from the store. And invariably someone says, "How are the egg nog sales this year?"

But my wife Marianne does a good job of bringing us back down to earth. We have a little vacation place in St. Martin that we go to and when we are down there we call it our "adult getaway." We bring our kids and their wives for one week. No small children. We go out to dinner together and we play together for a week. And whenever we start talking business Marianne always cuts in: "Remember, we're on vacation." But several of us always go off to the side and we talk business. It's awful hard not to bring business in, but that just proves the point that it is more than just a get-rich quick scheme. This is your life's work. It's your "bread and butter"—and it's fun!

If it wasn't more than the money, I might have quit long ago. I'm 61 years old. Why am I so enthused talking to you? Why am I doing this? Obviously, money is a measure of success. And obviously, I'm very, very proud that our business is successful, but that's not what I do it for. I work because I love it! And I bet if you talked to Jack Nicklaus it would be the same thing. He stopped working for the prize money long ago.

Q. How come you don't have 100 Stew Leonard's around the country?

A. I know there are professors that are teaching you how to multiply your company and get big and expand and leverage and all that. That could have been done with this company and it might still be done. But on the other hand lots of people look at me and shake their head and say "You are a unique situation that can't be duplicated." Sam Walton said that to me. I guess he's right that we're unique. Each day we try new things and change our ways of doing things. Now, can we duplicate that? It would be hard to get the type of people we have. It is great when everybody says, "Those people in Stew Leonard's . . .where did they find them?" Why try?

The money is not the reason to do it. Do you feel like eating another lunch right now? No, we just ate. Its the same with money. You become satisfied.The recognition? Well, sure everyone loves recognition. Marianne and I were invited to the Perry Como Christmas show at the Westbury Music Fair the other night by Mr. and Mrs. Balducci, the owners of the big New York food store. After the show, Mr. Balducci said, "I didn't tell you, but Perry Como is my personal friend. He lived next to me. He did his television special at my house and we're going backstage." We were thrilled to meet Perry Como. There was a young couple next to Perry Como and the woman shouts, "Stew Leonard!!" And her husband says, "Hey dad its Stew Leonard!!!" It was Perry Como's son and his wife who live in Westport and shop at our store. For the next five minutes all we did was shake hands. I was on cloud nine and needed a bigger hat size. That was all the recognition I'll ever need in my life if I live to be 100.

For that reason I would urge anybody to put their name on their business. I think the personal touch is very important . . . and its very rewarding to the owner as well.

For a long time now I've had a big sign in our store. It says: "Our mission is to create happy customers." If we spend all our time creating happy customers, everything else will follow. And the reason we don't have 30 stores, that 's never been our goal. But maybe the next generation will. And good luck to them.

I have a house in St. Martin's that is not seeing me as often as I want it to, and believe me its going to see me a lot more than it has in the past. And if we had 30 stores it probably wouldn't see me at all.

Q. How have customers changed from when you began in business?

A. When I first opened, my best selling items were: rich milk, ice cream, butter, bacon, any kind of red meat like roast beef. Today, those items have all been changed: the butter went to margarine, the ice cream went to fresh frozen yogurt, the rich milk went to skim milk and low fat milk, the meat went to fish and chicken. The customer has changed. The customer used to buy frozen peas and TV dinners. Now they buy fresh peas and they want fresh produce and they want everything fresh and they want to pick it out themselves. And they want to go to a salad bar where we have made their dinner for them. A salad bar which is as good as any fine restaurant. I never would have dreamed we'd be in that business.

Chinese foods are going gangbusters now. They are the new hot button. People's eating habits are constantly changing. There are many more men shopping in our store now because the women are working too and they are saying, "Why don't you pick up the stuff once in a while? I'm not going to be a slave when I go home tonight." I hear my own daughters saying it too!

So we're seeing people come in and pick up supper. They don't cook anymore. When they entertain, they get big platters and big trays. I think the multi-pak is the wave of the future. Getting the customer to buy several instead of one. Buy three get one free. Two for. Three for. There's got to be a way to get customers to buy a lot and put it in their pantry and let them inventory it instead of you. Then you can pass on the savings. Obviously, customer service is much better today. I think the customer is meeting, at least in our store, with much better trained people. Our people have been through Dale Carnegie courses. They have been through team member workshops and training. They have been taught to think "Yes, Yes, Yes." As the customer starts talking we start nodding, but not everyone thinks that way yet.

My daughter Jill recently went into a bookstore and bought six books. Came to $46. She paid for the books and they put them into a tissue paper bag. Jill said she could see the corner of the bag ripping as she picked it up. She looked over behind the salesperson and saw this beautiful plastic coated shopping bag with handles on it. She was planning to go walking through the mal, so she said to the clerk, "Can I have one of them?" And he said, "No, those are for our good customers." She said, "I just bought $46 worth of books. Aren't I a good customer?" And the salesman throws the bag at her. "Oh, ok, I guess you win." The dummy gave away a book bag, but because of poor training probably lost the customer to a competitor.

We've talked about pricing, volume, quality, motivation and family. But in the end it all comes down to customer service. If you don't have great people you can't build a great company. That's why we're continually searching for people with a good attitude. The other day I received this letter from an employee:

Dear Stew,

When I was promoted to recruiting manager of Stew Leonard's a few years ago I'll never forget your words: "Remember Chris, the most important thing to look for during an interview with a potential new team member is a good attitude. It's easy to teach people skills, but it's awfully hard to change a person's attitude."

A week ago, I interviewed a 19 year old boy for the produce department. He was on his very best behavior and passed every test. I then sent him to our Produce Manager, Martin Aarons, for the final interview which he also passed.

Last night I called him to give him the good news that he had been accepted for the job. I started the conversation off by explaining that I had called twice earlier in the day.

He immediately became annoyed and sarcastically said, "You must not listen very well, lady. I told you I had other commitments after school."

After receiving his put down, I began to imagine him talking to a customer saying, "You must not listen very well lady. I told you the string beans were over in the corner!"

Little things mean a lot. If only he had realized how important it is to think before he spoke.

With that, I politely said that the reason I was calling was to tell him that we were very sorry but we didn't have a job for him.

                    Chris Arnette

As bad as I feel for the young man not getting the job, I must compliment Chris for doing exactly the right thing. Our customers come first!

HELP!

HELP! INTRODUCTION

Companies which practice "tough selling" have satisfied customers. On the other hand . . .

I was standing in the Eastern Air Line counter line in Kansas City. The woman in charge had an argument with every customer.

"It's not my fault the plane is 15 minutes late. I don't fly the plane."

"This is a special fare ticket. There is no way to change it."

"It would help if you'd have your ticket ready for me."

One by one customers were chastised, ridiculed, made to feel unwelcome.

When it was my turn I started the conversation:

"Congratulations!"

She looked up, startled and said, "Congratulations? What for?"

"This must be your last day," I said.

"My last day? Why?"

"Well," I answered, "my wife always told me she could hardly wait until the last day we were in business. She would use that day to tell all the customers she disliked what she **really** thought of them because it wouldn't make any difference after that day. I figure the reason why you are making everyone so unhappy is because it's your last day. Is that right?"

She glared at me, stamped my ticket and I moved on . . .

Six months later, newspaper headline:

"Eastern declares bankruptcy."

HELP! QUOTES

"Rule #1: The customer is always right. Rule # 2: If the customer is wrong, reread Rule #1." — **Philosophy of Stew Leonard's supermarkets.** (see Stew Leonard interview in Wow! Chapter)

Tom Haggai on the IGA philosophy of "Hometown Proud"

"We are a community citizen. We care about the community. We are going to try to have a store that demonstrates how much we care. It is going to be pleasant and bright and a good place to sit around. We'll have someone who carries your groceries out.

Whether you shop with us or not, we're going to care about this town. We're not going to think that you owe us business. We're going to earn your business and thank you for letting us be here."

(Tom Haggai is CEO of IGA, one of the largest chain of retail supermarkets in the country. "Hometown Proud" is a marketing theme of IGA. See Tom Haggai interview in the "Organize!" chapter.)

"It is not enough merely to exist. It's not enough to say, 'I'm earning enough to live and to support my family. I do my work well. I'm a good father. I'm a good husband. I'm a good churchgoer.' That's all very well. But you must do something more. Seek always to do some good, somewhere. Every man has to seek in his own way to make his own self more noble and to realize his own true worth. You must give some time to your fellowman." — **Albert Schweitzer**

CUSTOM CARS

When Henry Ellis, a wealthy member of the English Parliament, decided to buy a car he went to the factory, told them his requirements and they delivered his order.

The year was 1894 and Ellis was the first person to drive an automobile in England. Today his hand-built car is on display in the Science Museum in London. A rarity, the first car to drive on primitive English roads.

In the 1900s, Henry Ford decided hand-built was definitely **not** the way to go and invented the assembly line. One worker, one job. One machine, one job. When told customers were asking for bright colors in their new cars, Ford's answer became legendary: "Give them any color they want. As long as it's black." Change was rare not only with Ford but also the other Big Two automakers.

Until 1955.

At the Toyota manufacturing plant in Japan, Taiichi Ohno, the company's production chief, came up with a revolutionary new way of making cars. Made-to-order for the customer. If Ohno had known the 1894 Englishman, he could have called it "The Henry Ellis Special."

In their book, "The Machine That Changed The World," writers James Womack, Daniel Jones and Daniel Roos explained how Toyota repositioned the responsibility of the manufacturer and retailer. Toyota gave customers what **customers** wanted (instead of what the company wanted).

Ohno researched the information his engineer Eiji Toyoda brought back from a 90 day observation tour of Ford Motor Company's River Rouge plant in Detroit. Together they decided mass production was **not** the answer.

Ohno organized his workers into teams. He told them to decide how to put the car together.

What were the results?

He used only half the human effort, half the manufacturing space, half the tool investment and half the engineering hours.

And that's only the manufacturing.

What happens when the car reaches the Japanese dealer?

Let's first tell you about the American car dealer.

Half of them have a big lot with a big inventory with big interest payments due every day the cars are not sold.

Most of them can only order the hottest designs and styles if they also agree to take others that are **not** selling well.

Most have a sales force that know little or nothing about how the car works.

Most — practically all — never see the customer after the sale.

Most have sales meetings infrequently. Unscheduled. Mostly crisis oriented.

Most are still selling cars the way their predecessors were a generation ago. High pressure. Rock 'em and sock 'em.

EXAMPLE #1: We recently visited a car dealer. We had purchased the same make the last three times. But this was a new dealer. He did not know us. He took our keys "for the mechanic's test drive." That was the last we saw of the keys till we forced him to return them to us.

We discussed a trade-in-price which started off at a ridiculous 10 percent of our car's selling price. We said we were insulted. His answer: "How about $1,000 more?" And when we expressed indignation, the classic closing phrase: "'All right, tell us what it would take for us to make the deal."

By then I was so unhappy I suggested an even swap — his new car for my four year old one.

Before he answered, we got up and left. The salesman followed us to our car yelling increased prices as we drove away: "Would you make the deal if we give you an extra thousand? **How about an extra two thousand . . .**"

We spent a few hundred dollars for a tune up at a competing dealer and kept the car an extra year.

EXAMPLE #2: We next visited another automobile dealer. While there, we noticed the showroom cars had stickers saying, "Ask about our Citicorp leasing program. Save hundreds of dollars."

And so we said to the salesman, "Tell us about your Citicorp leasing program that will save us hundreds of dollars."

He looked shocked. He said, "How did you know about that?"

We pointed to the stickers on the windows of the cars in his showroom.

He quickly ran to each car and ripped off the stickers. Returning with crumpled papers in his hand he explained, "That promotion ended last week!"

But what if we wanted to lease the car today?

Well, we would have to pay $100 a month more.

And what if we asked why we couldn't have the lease deal that was on the cars when we came into his showroom.

"Well, then I'd ask you, 'Where were you last week?'"

We sighed and left . . .

A recent Gallup Poll identifying professions for their ethical standards and honesty said that car salesmen were at the bottom of the list with only five percent of the people saying they were "ethical and honest." While this perception is certainly wrong about many car salesmen, there are enough bad apples to make many American customers suspicious and resentful.

Now, let's see how the Japanese car dealer works.

No big lots because land is scarce in Japan. Only a few samples. That's OK because, as you know from the above paragraphs, everything is made to order.

The salesman is paid on a **group** commission. All sales are added together.

Each car division has its own selling force.

Each dealership has 7-8 people trained in everything about the car. How it work. Advantages. Disadvantages.

Sales meetings start and end **every** day.

Let us follow a Japanese car salesman as he plans his day.

He knows whom he will see that day because the dealership has a profile of every household in their geographic area.

He goes door to door. He introduces himself. He fills out questionnaires about each and every family member. How many cars do they have? What features? How many children? Their ages.

All this data is put on a computer and a plastic "membership" card printed and mailed to each person in the household of car-owning age.

When someone in this family is interested in a car, they come to the dealership and put their membership card in a computer. The screen shows all the information the salesman has previously taken and suggests, based on that customer's demographics and psychographics, the car that best fits their profile.

If the customer is interested, he talks it over with members of the sales team.

The customer chooses what he wants, how he wants it. Each car is custom ordered — and delivered within a few weeks! (Shades of Henry Ellis).

The salesman takes care of everything. Yes, everything. Car insurance, parking permits (some Japanese cities require permits for bringing the car into the gridlock traffic).

The salesman also provide a warranty. Not for a specific time and/or miles but a warranty that never ends.

Have a problem with your insurance company?

Tell your salesman. He fights the battle for you and gives you a loaner while your car is repaired.

What they are developing is a long term relationship. Customers become part of the "Toyota Family." Salesmen send birthday cards, condolence cards, constantly keeping in touch.

When was the last time **you** received a phone call from your automobile dealer after you bought the car asking if everything was OK? Hasn't happened to me with the last four cars I bought.

"The only way to escape your car sales agent in Japan," said one customer, "is to leave the country."

Perhaps the U.S. car manufacturer is waking up. Says Ford's chairman Donald Petersen: "If we aren't customer driven, our cars won't be either."

Ford **has** changed and now surveys nearly 3 million customers a year to find out what they like and don't like about their cars.

HELP ME!

Ken Erdman, a direct mail consultant in Philadelphia, was shopping in a major department store. His wife had chosen some gifts but could find no one around to write up the sale. In desperation, Ken went to the center aisle and yelled at the top of his voice, "Help! Help! Help!"

He was quickly surrounded by security staff who asked what was the problem.

"No problem," said Ken. "I just want some help. Can you take care of me?"

In another chapter we talked about the number one wish people want from their jobs is "a feeling of being in on things."

One way to have your people involved is to ask **them** for help.

MANAGEMENT BY WALKING AROUND

Tom Peters, author of "In Search Of Excellence," champions his MBWA theory of Management By Walking Around.

The president of Federal Express visits his mechanics at airports. Aren't they the ones responsible for making sure the planes take off on time to make sure Federal Express maintains its high delivery percentage?

At Hyatt hotels, senior executives, including the president, put in time as bellhops.

Wayne Alderson was named vice president of operations of a steel mill near Pittsburgh, Pennsylvania. He was appointed after a bitter 84 day strike and a loss of $6 million.

First thing he did: Learned the names of each of the 300 workers. He walked in the plant to talk to the workers. Management safety helmets were white. Workers were black. He painted his black.

He thanked them for working with him. Most were amazed and wondered about his ulterior motive. One worker finally asked, "Why are you doing this?"

His answer: "Why not?"

A religious person, he led a weekly chapel meeting. The workers, first doubtful, then amazed, finally accepting, found their performance soaring. "He made us feel valuable" said one laborer.

In 12 months, productivity soared an astonishing 64 percent simply because Alderson gave the people that worked with him "love, dignity and respect."

Absenteeism disappeared. Sales rose 400 percent. The steel mill earned an extra $6 million in profits.

The firm made so so much money it was sold. The new management told Alderson he could no longer meet with the men. He could no longer pray with the men in the chapel. Alderson insisted. He was fired.

A short time later the plant closed after losing $70 million.

Alderson is doing well. He is a consultant and firms seek him out for help with labor.

DIFFERENT KINDS OF SERVICE

Another major problem with some sales personnel is they do not follow through. They tell the customer something will happen — and it does not.

It can be the insurance salesman scheduling a physical in your office at 3 o'clock. And no one shows up.

It can be the delicatessen that promises the party tray at your home at 5 PM. And nobody comes.

It can be the clothing shop that promises your tailoring will be ready Monday morning. And when you show up they say, "Oh, sorry. Won't be ready till tomorrow."

The Forum Company in Boston says, "The principal reason customers shift from one supplier to another is lousy service." Not price. Not quality. But service.

But good service keeps me coming back. For example:

• Top Notch resort in Stowe, Vermont. The first time we made a reservation we called on the way saying a snow storm would delay our arrival until about 10 that night. They said that was fine.

When we finally arrived, the last ones to show up for the evening, the room clerk looked up and said, "The Raphels are here! The Raphels are here!" The people behind the desk applauded, smiled and said, "We knew you'd make it . . ."

How do you think that made us feel?

• The room clerk in the Birmingham, Alabama Hyatt who asked if I wanted "a smoking or non-smoking room." Since this was one of the first times that was offered, I asked if there was really a difference.

Her answer: "Are you kidding? Do you want to go to sleep at night and suddenly smell that tobacco smell that makes you cough and wheeze and keeps you up all night? No sir! You want a fresh, clean, smells-nice room where you wake up ready to take on the world!"

• The waiter at Brennan's in New Orleans who told me, "Mr. Brennan would like you to have an after-dinner drink as a favor to him."

A favor to **him**? You bet. And how. And tell him I think of him often (or would from that moment on).

• Oliver, the doorman at Chicago's Continental Plaza, who opened the taxi as I was arriving for a seminar with the greeting, "How are you? We've been waiting for you!"

At last — recognition. About time people realized how

important I was.

I tipped him generously, and as I walked into the hotel, he opened the next taxi and cried out, "How are you? We've been waiting for you!"

All he did was . . . make money.

• A-Action Mobile Window Tinting in Orlando, Florida that will tint your car windows in your driveway. Just call.

• The Massachusetts firm that offers oil changes and tire checks while you're on vacation.

Can there be too much service? Not in Tough Times.

Well, once in a while . . .

I read recently of a woman in New Jersey who won $250,000 in the state lottery. When her Social Security check arrived, she mailed it back, explaining she no longer needed it.

The checks continued to arrive. She wrote back to no avail. She wrote her congressman and two U. S. Senators asking what she could do to get off the Social Security rolls.

All responded to her request assuring her they would do everything in their power to see she **continued to receive** her social security benefits.

TOUGH TIMES IN SWITZERLAND

Surviving in Tough Times means not only holding on to your job but doing so much business you create new jobs and cut down the national unemployment figures. Our favorite story on employment was told to us by Economics Nobel Prize Laureate James Tobin of Yale University. He recalled the time when he served on President Kennedy's Council of Economic Advisors. There was a meeting in Washington which he chaired with ministers from countries around the world. The subject was Unemployment And What Your Country Is Doing About It. Each of the ministers told how they were handling the problem. Finally the minister from Switzerland spoke. Tobin asked him how his country was handling the unemployed. The minister answered, "Well, I really don't know. But when I get back home, I'll invite both of them over for dinner and we'll talk about it."

INTRODUCTION TO SOL PRICE INTERVIEW

Most retailers view the customer with suspicion.

The customer must be cajoled, coddled, wheedled. The customer is always looking for a gimmick, an angle, a break, a discount, a sale. The customer wants to be pampered, but will return merchandise on a whim. Even if the merchandise fits right. Even if the merchandise has been worn!

In short, the customer is a dangerous foe and must be treated with apprehension and a touch of disdain.

Wait!

What if those retailers have it wrong.

What if the true calling of the retailer is to be the purchasing agent of the consumer. The retailer would then try to buy merchandise at the lowest possible price from the manufacturer, charge the bare minimum markup to the consumer and stand behind the quality and workmanship of the product.

Is this a prescription for economic suicide?

No, thought Sol Price, not if volume is high enough.

Sol Price started the warehouse club concept in America. Customers at Price Club would become members of a buyers' club established for their benefit. Price's dream was that he could give his customers the lowest possible retail price by limiting selection, advertising and use of credit. Because of the small margins he would have to do a huge volume in each location.

And it worked! Customers include people from every walk of life who want high quality at the lowest possible prices — even the rich and famous. Customers include Marilyn Quayle, Marlon Brando and Ernest Borgnine.

And now a typical Price Club does one hundred million dollars in sales per year (Yes! Count them. Eight zeros. $100,000,000).

Read on and find out Price's thoughts today on the industry he helped spawn.

SOL PRICE INTERVIEW

Q. Do you conduct your business any differently when the headlines say we are in a recession?

A. I think there is no question that business is much softer. People are buying more and more of what they need and less and less of what they would like to have. In our business it is even accentuated a little bit more because we rely so much on our wholesale trade. There is no question that sales are softer than they were.

We look upon the recession as a problem but also as an opportunity. The depressed real estate market provides us with unique opportunities to acquire land at substantially lower prices than would have been the case a couple of years ago.

Q. Shouldn't a business like yours prosper during a recession?

A. I'm not sure I would use the word "prosper." When the psychological attitude of people is that they are just not excited about spending money, it affects us too. I think to a great extent we may suffer less than others because of our low prices and we have so much of our business in basics.

Q. Stew Leonard and you both say that you run your business in similar fashions, that you want to have high value and try to have high quality.

A. Well that is the same bull that everybody says. Talk is cheap. It is really execution that counts. Everybody says they have great prices and great quality. Did you ever hear anybody say we sell crap and we charge a lot for it?

Q. Are you charging the lowest price to the consumer or are you really charging what the consumer will bear?

A. My philosophy has always been you sell as cheap as you can, not what the traffic will bear. That's pretty fundamental. People who advertise a lot can get away with higher prices, but we depend totally upon the reputation and credibility that we have with our customers. We don't rely upon promotional advertising to make the sale.

For instance, supermarkets give bargains every week in the newspaper and have to buy their customer back week after week. We don't do that. Obviously we have to have great credibility. You have to get to the point where the people come to you and have the attitude when they walk in that, "I can buy whatever I want here because I know that they are giving me a great value."

Q. And so you really are geared towards value?

A. That is the basis of the whole industry.

Q. Are you opposed to advertising in general?

A. For thirty years I've always said the best advertising is unsolicited testimonials. The worst advertising is the stuff that costs you so much that you have to raise your prices because of your message. I do have a philosophical problem with conventional advertising that is simply a cynical message to try to make people believe that they are getting something that they really aren't.

Q. Do you think that is the fault of advertising agencies?

A. An advertising agency is just like a lawyer. It is there to render a service for the client, and if the client doesn't have the right philosophic approach, it's the client's fault, not the agency's fault.

Q. You send newsletters to your club members. Do you do that as an advertising marketing vehicle or something different?

A. It is part of an obligation that we have to our people. We think it's a good way of communicating with our people. I'm not saying advertising per se is bad. The real question is what's the purpose of it. Is it to give a message or to get somebody to buy something that they really don't need and make them think that they are trying to get some kind of a big bargain, when they aren't?

If we spent 3 percent of sales on advertising, there would be no profit left.

Q. Do you view supermarkets as competitors?

A. We view everybody as a competitor — supermarkets, department stores, specialty stores. Everybody is a competitor. Are supermarkets worse than others? I'm not sure. They do more advertising.

Q. Do you believe in promoting from within your organization?

A. Very much so. You should not become so insular that you never get exposed to other people because you get a rigidity built into the company. But, generally, yes, it is very important for all your people to feel that there is opportunity. You tend to get people who have been exposed to your way of doing things, which is very important especially if you're doing something that is somewhat unconventional.

I'll tell you a story about a guy I hired many, many years ago from Sears. He worked in our hardware department. I was running Fedmart and we believed in limited selections. I came down to San Antonio where he worked and saw he had three different sizes of 3 in 1 oil. One sold for 19 cents, one for 29 cents and one for 49 cents. I said, "George, if I could prove to you that you're losing volume by having the 19 cent can would you eliminate it?" He said, "Yes." So I said, "Well, if you didn't have it, out of ten customers that would buy the 19 cent can how many do you think wouldn't buy the 29 cent or 49 cent can?" He's said that nine out of ten would buy the next size.

I added up the increase in volume. He said, "Boss, that is right." So I said, "How about if we eliminated the 29 cent can?" And again I convinced him we would do more volume.

I came back in six months and visited his department and saw he was back to the three sizes. He was not about to lose a sale. He did not understand our way of doing business.

If you educate your people properly and they understand your philosophy, it is much easier to promote those people than it is to get people who are coming from conventional retailers that have to learn a whole new philosophy.

Q. *So you are teaching them a system, a way of doing business?*

A. We are teaching them a philosophy.

Q. *How do you motivate them to provide excellent customer service?*

A. Pretty much by paying well and trying to teach the golden rule. How you treat them is how they end up treating the customer.

Q. *There is no direct measurement of customer service?*

A. No. The way you find out is how many people renew their membership.

Q. *And if the renewal rate is not satisfactory in a particular store?*

A. Then you have to look in to it to see why that is. Obviously you get signals way before then. You get customer complaints, complaints from other employees. You get a variety of things.

Q. *Is your way of doing business, the warehouse concept, applicable to other industries?*

A. Take a look around you. Home Depot is a spin off from us. So are office clubs, such as Staples. Whether or not they are as fundamentally sound as we are, who knows. Time will tell.

Q. *Would you like to get into other industries or are you busy enough with what you are doing now?*

A. We've moved into many things, into one hour photo finishing, optical service. We have a couple of pharmacies, we are starting with fresh meat and have our own little bakeries. Over the years we've done a lot of that. We've gone into travel.

Q. *What criteria do you use for hiring?*

A: I've always felt that I was interested #1 in integrity, #2 intelligence, #3 industry and #4 ingenuity. If a person has those qualities, I'm not concerned about whether they have the technical knowledge.

Q. *One of the things that you focus on is being an agent to the customers and making them happy. Are there times when customers are wrong, and how do you handle those situations?*

A. It all depends on what you mean by wrong. If you're talking about an individual situation of a customer tearing open a box or something like that, you handle it on an ad hoc basis. We always try to talk about the golden rule and use good judgement.
  There are many customers that want things that we're not prepared to give them and that is the basis of our whole philosophy which is the intelligent loss of sales. If they want you to be open certain hours or they want more selection or they want a variety of things, we're prepared to say that is a sale we're going to lose.

Q. *Can't someone be successful trying to imitate you, but not doing it with a club concept and not charging an entry fee?*

A. Staples and Home Depot don't charge fees. Nobody in our industry is doing that yet, but I suspect that somebody will try. My guess is if they do that, they're going to move into advertising, they're going to move in the credit cards, they're going to move in a variety of things and the pricing won't be as good.

Q. *Do you see a time when Price Club could eliminate the fee?*

A. I don't think so. But forever is a long time.

Q. *What is the reason you still need the fee?*

A. There are a variety of reasons. The person who pays you the fee is making a commitment. If you don't just take that money and squirrel it away and say it is pure profit, if you take that money and put it back in to the shelf price, what you're doing is making sure the more people buy, the more return they are getting on their $25 membership fee.

Q. *Would you ever do anything for frequent buyers or is that against your philosophy of offering things at the lowest price?*

A. I'm not sure we would do it on the basis of frequent buyer. We obviously would consider, should consider and are considering the prospect of giving those members who cost less for you to serve, some kind of way of giving back some of their money. Obviously somebody paying $25 a year who spends $10,000 a year is getting more benefit than the guy who is paying $25 and only spending $500 a year.

Q. You don't reward that first person yet, but you're thinking about it?

A. He is rewarded by the fact that his $25 membership buys him more. The fellow who spends $500 a year and pays $25 is paying a 5 percent premium. The guy that spends $10,000 and pays $25 is paying a .25 percent premium. The smaller buyer is subsidizing him. In effect he is getting some advantage. Now should we give him some additional advantage? We always keep thinking about that, talking about it.

Q. If you did something like that would you do it in one of your stores or would you roll it out?

A. We generally try things first and see how they go.

Q. Have you changed your merchandising concepts much since you first started?

A. Not the basic concept. Obviously we're doing a lot of things now that we didn't do when we began.

Q. Are you offering more of the more expensive items now?

A: You mean things like computers, sure.

Q. That's been dictated by what customers want?

A. It's dictated by a variety of things. Mostly, we hope by the ingenuity and merchandising talents of our buyers.

Q. Do you see a time when it would make sense for you to accept credit cards?

A. We're looking at that all the time. I don't know whether you're aware of the problem with credit cards. There's a federal law that says you can't charge the customer for using the credit card. You can give them a discount, but you can't say this is our shelf price and we have to pay a point or a point and a half to the creditor, so if you want to use your credit card we're going to up charge you the points. That is against the law.

We believe there is a flaw in the credit card business as it applies to us. We've had companies approach us and say they won't charge us for the merchandise we sell and our customers will get the card for free. What we would be doing and what we have to evaluate is: Do we want to expose our members to a situation where the only way the credit card can continue to be available to them is if a substantial number of them have to go into the credit part of the credit card and pay 19-20 percent interest? That we find hard to swallow.

Q. The only way the credit cards are going to make money is by charging that 19 percent?

A. The only way they do it is by the number of people that don't pay within the 30 days, who go into credit. The only way they can survive is that way.

Q. Do you have any lessons that you would want to impart to would-be entrepreneurs?

A. I suppose the only real lesson is that if you want to have a satisfactory relationship with the person with whom you're dealing you have to be prepared to give before you get.

TOUGH SELLING FOR TOUGH TIMES

5

REWARD!

REWARD! INTRODUCTION

Everyone wants to be **remembered** — and to be **rewarded** — on a regular basis.

Everyone. As a sales or business person should you seek ways to reward your customers? Sure.

But you should also seek ways to reward the people that work with you every day.

Not just with money (that helps) but with recognition.

REMEMBER: In Tough Marketing Times, everybody remembers the business that remembers them.

REWARD! QUOTE

"The rewarded customer buys, multiplies, and comes back."
   Dr. Michael LeBoeuf

REWARD! STORY

There's an old joke abut two friends, Bill and Pete.

Bill goes to Pete to borrow some money and Pete turns him down.

Incensed, Bill says, "How can you turn me down? When you were having troubles with your wife, wasn't I the one who brought the two of you back together? When your daughter wanted to get into college, wasn't I the one that wrote the best recommendation? When you wanted an introduction to sell your product to the biggest firm in town, didn't I set up the appointment and you made the sale?"

Pete thought about that for a while, nodded his head in agreement and then said, "But what have you done for me lately?"

WAYS TO SAY "THANK YOU"

For forty years, we owned and operated a retail clothing mall named Gordon's (after my in-laws) in Atlantic City.

Every Thanksgiving we gave away a present to everyone who shopped in our store.

The reactions varied. Some said, "What's this for?" Or, "Did I buy that?"

We answered, "It's Thanksgiving. It seems the right time of the year to say 'thanks' for shopping with us. I'm sure we say 'thank you' every time you shop. I hope we do. But it just seems right at Thanksgiving that we tell you again how much we appreciate your business. This is just a small way of saying 'thanks.'"

In our buying trips for the store we would look for a great little gift item with perceived value. "How much do you think this is worth?" was the question we asked ourselves. If the answer was ten times more than the cost, it was chosen.

We made sure it was **not** merchandise we sold in our store. Otherwise Perceived Value became Real Value.

Example: A supermarket ran an ad giving away violets to every customer at Easter. Good move. Until you opened to an inside page and found you could also buy the violets in the store for 99 cents. Does that mean the customer was only worth 99 cents?

A reverse of that is what we did on Memorial Day. **We** contacted a local florist and placed an order for 500 miniature clay pots with two inch high baby trees. **Everyone** who shopped in the store received a tree to take home and plant. The cost of each tree was under a dollar. The value received from the astonished customer was impossible to measure. How much was the plant worth? One dollar? Three dollars? Five dollars? Answer: Whatever the customer **thought** it was worth. Which was always much higher than our actual cost.

One Christmas, through a friend, we contacted the mayor of Norfolk Island in the Pacific Ocean nearly two thousand miles from the nearest land of Australia. Norfolk is famous for three reasons:

1. Their postage stamps. The worldwide sale of these collector items for philatelists pay for municipal services in lieu of taxes. (Now that's an idea!)

2. The final home of the descendants of the Bounty. (Remember Fletcher Christian and his mates throwing Captain Bligh overboard?)

3. The origin of the Norfolk Pine, thought by many as the ideal

Christmas tree.

We had the mayor of Norfolk Island write a note to "The Customers of Gordon's In Atlantic City" in which he told the history of the Norfolk Pine.

We reduced the letter and placed it in a small pot with a miniature Norfolk Pine purchased from our local florist. We placed an advance order for 1,000 trees for the Christmas season. We felt this would last us the five selling weeks from Thanksgiving to Christmas.

We ran out the first week!

Everyone wanted the baby Norfolk Pine Tree. We had to air freight a special shipment of a few thousand more trees to meet the demand. Friends told friends who told friends and all came to shop in our store because of the free little Norfolk Pine Christmas Tree.

We never told anyone we were giving away the trees. We never advertised the fact. But the word quickly spread. And more and more customers arrived simply because of the "free tree."

We call these "gifts" Added Value. Added Value is the unexpected, unadvertised, unasked for "extra" you give your customer. The key to Added Value is to make sure you do **not** advertise, you do **not** promote, you do **not** tell anyone about it until they receive it.

In Tough Selling Times, the customer that continues to buy from you is the customer that knows you appreciate their business. Because you tell them. And Reward them.

OUR FAVORITE PROMOTION: THE GORDON'S GOLD CARD

The idea was first planted by a formula I learned from John Groman, one of the founders of Epsilon, one of America's largest data base companies and a division of American Express. John is an idea man and lecturer on data base marketing around the world. He once told me, "There are only three ways of doing more business. Here they are:

1. Have More Customers.

2. Have Your Customers Come In More Often.

3. Have Them Buy More When They Come In."

I have used those three guidelines since the first time he taught them to me because they are true and, more important, they work!

One day, trying to figure how to create more business in our shops, I ran across John's Three Principles Of Doing More Business as I was about to leave for a series of seminars in Australia.

I was excited about going on the trip not only because of seeing friends in Australia but also because I had received two round trip first class tickets for wife Ruth and myself . . . free!

I had these free tickets as a **reward** from an airline for flying so many miles with them. I was one of their valued Frequent Flyers. The airline was rewarding me for being a good customer.

But how was I rewarding my customers for being good customers?

If I could think of a way that would not only reward them but also have them spend more money with me, I would do more business.

If the airlines made it work with Frequent Flyer programs why not make it work with a Frequent Buyer program at Gordon's?

I assembled the Airline Frequent Flyer programs. I belong to ten, so their material was available. Marriott was just beginning their Honored Guest program for their hotel chain so I wrote for information. Their success, by the way, prompted almost **all** the hotel chains to copy the idea. My wallet is full of cards that tell me I belong to Inter Continental's Six Continents Club, the Adam's Mark Gold Mark Club, the Hilton Honors Program, The Hyatt Platinum Passport . . .

I also picked up the latest material from the major credit card companies (Diner's gives their best customers gifts!) and what the gasoline companies offered.

I read every brochure, pamphlet, letter and picked out the sentences that appeared in most of them. Why take the time to create a new selling package when it was already done?

Here's one of the great sentences that almost **every** Frequent Buyer/Flyer program uses. Copy it for your future Reward program for **your** business:

"Your association with Gordon's and your annual volume of business with us places you in a unique group which requires and appreciates special recognition."

How could you not continue reading **that** letter?

We then went through our customer computer printout and set an arbitrary number of $1,000 as the minimum amount of purchases you had to spend in our store in one year to receive a Gordon's Gold Card. We selected nearly 500 customers. We now had 500 customers that gave us more than one and a half million dollars in business every year!

Yes, yes, I know that 500 times $1,000 is $500,000. But remember that was the **minimum**. Some of the customers spent $2,000 or $4,000 a year with us. One customer the previous year spent $12,500 in clothing. (We would have given her **ten** cards if she asked.)

It was the 80/20 rule staring at us. In fact, less than 20 percent of our customers accounted for 80 percent of our volume!

We printed attractive gold-on-white plastic cards with each customer's name in gold. We mailed them a complete package including a letter, a free lunch at the Alley Deli restaurant (once a month), a gift certificate to say "thanks" for being a Gold Card member and the all important questionnaire to find out more about each customer.

The letter said they would receive the following:

1. Instant recognition.

2. The Alley Deli free lunch every month.

3. Advance announcements. First class mail for all store mailers instead of bulk rate.

4. Birthday present for them **and** their spouse.

5. Unadvertised special offers. We began a monthly mailing to only Gold Card customers with outstanding specials. Cost: $500 a month or one dollar for each one mailed. Our lowest sales return from these monthly mailings was $4,000. The highest return in

sales from these monthly mailings was $23,500!

6. Gift selection and complimentary mailings. No charge for postage and handling when they mailed gifts.

7. Bonus points. (More on that in a few paragraphs.)

8. A questionnaire which customers filled out and returned because it had their birthday — and their spouse's birthday — which we needed to send them a gift on that special day. They also gave us other valuable information including what designers they bought. What they liked best about the shops. What they wanted us to carry that we did not. Where they read or saw our ads.

We quickly discovered that 75 percent of our best customers listened to **one** radio station. Since there are 12 radio stations in our area and we never knew which one to choose for advertising, our customers told us! And since future customers would be listening to this same station, that's where we put our advertising dollars.

We found out by rewarding our customers, they rewarded us!

We added a P.S. to the bottom of the letter saying, "Since we always like happy endings, we'll add one to this letter. We've enclosed a $15 gift certificate in your name to use in any of our shops . . ."

No minimum purchase. No, "If you buy, you get . . ." The Fifteen Dollars was **free**.

We have consistently found out your best customers will **not** take advantage of you. We were not surprised to discover that our average sale was $50 when the $15 gift certificate was used. Translation: A profit on **every** gift certificate used.

The Gold Card was directly responsible for giving us a big increase in business.

BONUS POINTS

We kept track of our Gold Card Customers' sales from their sales slips. They received a gift certificate at Thanksgiving (naturally) for holiday shopping. The gift certificates amounted to about 5 percent of their purchases. But we didn't say that. We said, "Each dollar is one bonus point. If you earn 250 to 500 points, you receive a gift certificate for $25. If you earn 501 to 750 points you receive a gift certificate for $50." All the way to a maximum gift certificate of $100.

The first year we gave away about $5,000 in gift certificates.

Which was responsible for $25,000 in business.

Would we have done part of this "extra" $25,000 in business anyway?

Yes.

Would we have done all that "extra" $25,000 in business without the Frequent Buyer plan? Absolutely, positively, unconditionally "No."

But the greatest reaction was . . . surprise! The letter, received months earlier with the promise of Bonus Points and gift certificates, was forgotten. All the customer knew was they opened up their mail one day and out came **free** gift certificates for merchandise.

What good feelings about our business!

What a story to tell their friends!

What a reason to come and shop with us when other businesses were complaining about . . . tough times!

MEETING WITH YOUR STAFF

Meet with your staff at least once a month. Once a week is better.

A survey taken by the University of Maryland asked employees "What do you want most from your job?"

Higher wages came in fourth.

The first, top-of-the-list requirement from most people that responded was, "A feeling of being in on things."

At your weekly meetings you have an agenda and you discuss what's happening in the coming weeks and months. You show your staff copies of print ads and have them listen to the radio commercials. You do this **before** the ads run so you can ask, "What do you think? Would you make any changes?"

Share your marketing/advertising/promotion ideas with the

people who are responsible for selling your merchandise. **Always** end each meeting by going around the room and calling on everyone by name asking if there's something else they want to add. They must feel part of the process.

We tell the story of the time we were in Memphis, talking to the Tennessee Grocers Association. Supermarkets have a very high turnover of personnel. We approached one owner and asked, "How many people do you have in your business?"

"I have 85 people working for me," he said.

"Well," we answered, "it's a shame most of them will leave you by the end of the year."

"What?" he said

"Didn't you say you had 85 people **working for you**?" we asked.

"Yes."

"Then most of them will leave you by the end of the year."

"Would you explain that please?" he asked.

"Sure, we said. "If you had told me you had 85 people working **with** you, then I would tell you hardly no one will leave. You see, everyone wants to work **with** someone. No one wants to work **for** someone."

You must also make sure your staff shares in rewards.

The obvious reward is money. We set up simple goals for each department. Everyone knew how much money their department did the previous year. If they had a certain percentage increase, they received a certain bonus. Higher increases, higher bonuses.

Every month we reviewed how each department was doing and how close each person was to a particular bonus goal.

The not-so-obvious rewards are Valued Memories.

For several years we closed the store for three days and took everyone on vacation!

We ran ads in the paper saying,"We're closed for the next three days because we're all going on our annual vacation!"

(That was the time of the year when we received the most applications. We were asked, "How can I work in **your** store?")

Once we went to Disney World. Another time we hired a special deluxe bus with built in TV, lounges, catered lunches and took everyone on a trip through Vermont to our favorite villages. Still another time we went to New Orleans, had breakfast at Cafe du Monde and dinners at famous French Quarter restaurants.

Lots of pictures. Many memories. People still talk about them. The money, though desired and wanted and appreciated, is soon forgotten.

The memories of the good times together are **never** forgotten.

THE GREATEST BUSINESS SECRET IN THE WORLD

Remember the scene in the Western movies where the camera panned to a close-up of the poster of the bank robber? At the top in big black letters was the word "Wanted!" Then the name. And then, in even bigger and blacker letters the word: "**Reward!**"

The reason was simple: Offer someone a reward for doing something and the response will be far greater than if you simply tell them you want something.

You want your salespeople to bring in more sales. You'll have them bring in more sales if you give them a **reward**!

You want more customers to come to your store or buy your product. They will come and buy more quickly if you also give them a **reward**!

We call this sales technique the Psychology of The Second Interest. Here's what it means:

You can have someone buy something you want them to buy if you **reward** them with something else they want to buy.

It's far easier to make a sale if you stop concentrating on the product **you** want to sell and, instead, offer something else **the customer wants.**

Which is why there are toys in crackerjack boxes.

Which is why supermarket openings feature a free Jeep and a Caribbean cruise on the front page of the ad just below the words "Grand Opening."

Which is why Procter and Gamble will give you $5 towards the latest Disney videotape if you buy one of their products and send in the box top.

People buy better, faster and quicker when you offer a reward.

THE FIVE REASONS PEOPLE DO NOT BUY

What are some of the reasons people do **not** buy? If we knew them would they help you come up with a reward that would make them **want** to buy?

Here are the five most common reasons why people say they do **not** buy what you have for sale. In these difficult times you hear them used more often than before.

Your assignment is to Free The Negative Five! Break their chains! If you know what they are and how they work, you can cast them aside.

1. **No need**
2. **No money**
3. **No hurry**
4. **No desire**
5. **No trust**

Let's take them one at a time and see how we can overcome these no-no-no-no-nos.

1. No Need

Joe Karbo took in $10 million because he answered his customers' needs. He offered them a book titled *The Lazy Man's Way To Riches*. Most people figure you have to work hard to make a million dollars. After all, less than one-half of 1 percent of the U.S. population are millionaires. But look, here's advertising copy that said if (1) you were lazy and (2) you wanted to be rich, read this book.

He offered his customers a reward.

2. No Money

We once sold clothing door-to-door. When customers told us they had no money, we said, "No problem. Just give us a dollar a week on your bill and we will pick it up from you every week." This doubled our volume the first year. We no longer picked up just the $1 on their account, we sold them new merchandise as well. And we told them what we would offer them in a weekly mailer with the items we would bring them *next* week.

It is a proven, guaranteed, never-fail fact that the more ways you give a customer to buy, the more they will buy. Cash. Charge. Credit. Layaway. Having "no money" is one of the easiest not-to-buy reasons to eliminate. Your reward: you don't pay for everything at once. A little at a time. Affordable.

3. No Hurry

Franklin Mint offered a limited number or reproductions of classic books bound in leather and numbered. When that number was reached, the too-late customer received their money back with a "Sorry, you didn't order in time" note. Will they order *faster* next time? Oh, yes!

Greenwich Workshop offers signed, limited edition prints from famous American artists to their 1,000+ distributors across the country. In the past, as soon as a new print was made available, it was oversold. Now dealers no longer write in what they want. They call and fax their orders. They know if they don't hurry, they have no inventory. No inventory, no sales, no reward.

Another way to create desire: Offer a reward. One of the above mentioned Greenwich Workshop retailers put together a Member-Get-A-Member program — a $25 gift certificate for every new customer a present customer brought to the store. In the first month five of the new customers made purchases totaling $9,204. Cost of the gift certificates and printing: $300.

I just received a pop-up calendar in the mail from a company that wants to see if I'm interested in pop-ups. They were very clever to make sure I didn't take advantage of them since the calendar they sent me was for 1988. Their thinking: If I wanted calendars for 1991, I'd have to order them. My thinking: I threw out the 1988 calendar. But if the sample had been 1991, I would have kept it on my desk because it was current. However, there was no calendar on my desk because they offered me no reward.

4. No Desire

Dr. Ernest Dichter, head of the Institute of Motivational Research, said when people come to a restaurant they are hungrier for *recognition* than they are for food.

Writer Robert Ringer says the best-selling headline he ever wrote was to promote Douglas Casey's best-selling book, *Crisis Investing*. Wrote Ringer: "Why You Will Probably Lose Everything In The Coming Depression."

The book sold 400,000 copies and was on *The New York Times* best-seller list for 15 weeks.

But when you create the desire, you must also supply the answer.

Story: German submarines were destroying Allied ships in World War I. The Allies called in a consultant. He said to heat the ocean to 180 degrees, which would force the Germans to surface the submarines and they then could be attacked.

The Navy thought this was a great idea and asked the consultant, "But how do we heat the ocean to that temperature?" Said the consultant, "I'm a consultant. I gave you the answer. You work out the details."

One way to create a desire is to appeal to someone's city, country or favorite sporting team. Any kind of tie-in generates increased bottom-line results.

There is a classic story of the Polish veteran from the town of Dryna who returned from World War II, and, because of the strain of combat, was mute. No one could get him to talk. One day he was in a veteran's hospital listening to a radio game of his hometown Dryna playing soccer against the traditional competitive city. In a hard fought battle, his team scored the winning goal. At that exact moment he jumped out of his bed and yelled, "We won!"

And never said anything again until the day he died.

5. No Trust

Ringer also tells the "most unsuccessful ad I ever wrote" was headlined "An Open Letter To Howard Hughes." But the product had absolutely nothing to do with Howard Hughes. No reward for reading.

It was a gimmick to have someone read the ad. And after they read the ad and found nothing in the ad that dealt with Howard Hughes, they stopped reading and stopped trusting.

A company in Dublin sent out a direct mail piece offering their laundry service. The company's reputation was good, their service excellent, but they received a pathetically small response to their letter. Oh, the name of the company was "Swastika Laundry Ltd." with a swastika symbol on their stationery. No amount of explaining that a "swastika" means "good luck" and is merely "a symbol in the form of a Greek cross" could develop a trust in their readers. The symbol was stigmatized.

By freeing the Negative 5 you will be better equipped to reward your current customers. Says Roger A. Enrico, president of Pepsico Worldwide Beverages: "If you are totally customer focused and you deliver the services your customers want, everything else will follow."

Free The Negative Five!

Offer a Reward!

TONY INGLETON INTRODUCTION

We were doing a seminar in Australia twelve years ago. Afterwards we met a rather persistent, enthusiastic, good-looking Australian. He said he was in the travel and entertainment business and loved our seminar and could we perhaps help him in his business and he would be so ever grateful for our input . . .

Tony Ingleton's enthusiasm and panache captivated us and we have been working with him ever since.

Tony has created the Presidential Card, a travel and entertainment card that is used by 140,000 Australians. The card is based on the principle of reward. The card gives discounts on meals (buy one meal and your second entree is free), hotels, entertainment (including Australia's largest movie chain) and travel. Members pay a yearly fee to belong.

Tony lives and works in Melbourne, Australia, which is a twenty hour plane ride to America. But Tony has spent 220 days, in over 40 separate trips, to Disneyland and Disney World in the United States. Disney's qualities of value and reward have inspired Tony and provided a foundation upon which he has built his business.

TONY INGELTON INTERVIEW

Q. How did your fascination with Disney begin?

A. Ever since I was a kid, I loved Disney. I loved buying the comics. When the Mickey Mouse Club started in 1956, it was my favorite television program. About 1960, when I was eighteen, I felt very sad because I actually thought that I had missed out on Disneyland. I thought you really had to be a child to get a benefit of going to Disneyland. Of course later I was to realize how wrong that was. I first visited Disneyland in 1978 when I was 36 years old.

The day I arrived it was drizzling with rain and the one attraction, featuring parts of the Carribean, which I really wanted to see was closed that morning for repairs.

And yet I had the happiest day of my life. I mean it was just fantastic. I was very apprehensive in a way, because when you build something up in your mind — in this case I had built this up 23 years — you feel very nervous. What happens if it's nothing like I thought it would be? But Disneyland was just so far ahead of my expectations, that it's hard to put into words.

Here's what surprised me most: The more I return to Disneyland, the more I enjoy the experience. Today I can go back to Disneyland for a day and not go on one ride. I get there at 10 o'clock in the morning, walk around all day, leave at eight o'clock at night. I've spent 10 hours there. And I think to myself when I leave, "Where did the 10 hours go?" It's just such a tremendous experience. Everyone that goes there is very happy.

Q. How did the influence of Disney affect your business?

A. What influenced my thinking with the Presidential Card, when I first was exposed to Disneyland, was that Disney was a genius. He understood people and what they wanted. He recognized people want quality in a package they can afford.

That's what I've tried to do with the Presidential Card. I changed the image of our program to provide something that was very high quality. I wanted people to say, "My God, that looks so expensive, that must cost 500 dollars a year to belong to that club." In reality, it costs about $70 to belong. Other competitive programs in Australia have a start up fees that are three times higher than the Presidential Card.

Q. You've been to Disneyland and Disney World several dozen times. How do you have so much time to travel?

A. Many people come to me and say, "I wish I had your lifestyle." Or, "I wish I could go to Disneyland as often as you do." The reality is that a lot of those people could do it. They have the perception that they have to work 9 to 5 five days a week, fifty weeks of the year. Some of them say, "I can't afford to take the time off from my business." But if they had a car accident tomorrow and were in the hospital for four weeks, somehow their business would survive.

I plan the periods that I'm going to be away traveling for enjoyment. I find that when I travel, I relax. I see things in a different light.

Q. Have you developed personal friendships with the Disney characters?

A. Because I've been to Disneyland and Disney World so often, I've developed friendships with the people who play the characters. I've had Mickey Mouse visit my house in Australia. And I mean **the** Mickey Mouse, the official Mickey Mouse that travels, representing Disney.

People ask me if I'm upset to meet the actual person playing the role of Mickey Mouse. It doesn't bother me because you really don't lose the illusion. It's not like seeing Mickey Mouse walking around without his head and having a real person's head sticking out of the costume. That might be a bit disillusioning I suppose. And when you go to Disneyland and you meet Mickey Mouse and the other characters, they still are playing a role which is very important to them.

The actors talk about Mickey Mouse as if he is a real person. They perceive that he is real. And who's to tell them they're wrong? Not me!

6

ORGANIZE!

ORGANIZE! INTRODUCTION

Most of us do not organize ourselves.

Most of us fall into a habit of doing what we did yesterday, the day before, the week before, the year before.

Most of us live life as it comes, not making changes in the Arabic tradition of "If Allah wanted it to change, it would change."

Most of the time you can get away with that.

Except now.

When times are tough in your business, your need to organize becomes compelling.

Organize? You have a difficult enough time just getting through the day. How can you organize, plan, establish goals? You're too busy putting out fires, surrounded by alligators in the swamp and haven't got the time to . . .what? Organize?

Take the time.

Each of you have a very special talent that is yours alone. How do you take that talent and make it work for you? If you do not straighten out your priorities, there will be no time left for your true talents to emerge.

"Each man has his own vocation," said Emerson. "The talent is the call. He can do something which is easy for him and good when it is done but which no other man can do."

So this is a call for listing your resources, establishing your goals, **organizing** what you want to get done. And how. And when!

ORGANIZE! QUOTE

"I'm continually asking myself: 'What is the best use of my time right now?' "

—Alan Lakein, time management consultant

YOUR OBITUARY

Someone comes to see you and says,"I'd like you to play a game with me."

You like to play games. "Sure," you say, "What do I do?"

He gives you a sheet of paper, a pen and explains the rules, "It's very simple. All you have to do is write your own obituary."

You are shocked, taken aback, not sure how to react.

"Write my own obituary? What for?"

"Because," he says, "You'll then see what you've accomplished with your life. So write down all your achievements, the goals you set and met. Above all, how you fulfilled yourself. Ready . . . start!"

THE HEADLINE TECHNIQUE

We visited a friend who owned a large trucking firm. His office was at the end of a large room facing a series of desks where his traffic people worked. We talked with him — or rather tried to talk to him.

Every few minutes one of the people behind the desk would come in and spend a few minutes telling a long story about a particular trucking problem.

After a half hour we asked how could he accomplish anything during the day when he was constantly interrupted to make someone else's decision. We suggested he try "The Headline Technique" and explained how it worked: Starting the next morning, when any of his staff came into his office they should start the conversation with a headline and not a long story.

If someone says to you, "The peaches due to be shipped next month will be a week late," say, "Thanks" and you know you have time to handle that problem. If someone else says,"The building is burning down and your office is next," well, that requires faster action.

The next morning he told the staff of the new Headline Technique. For a while, some would still come in, start a long story and he would stop them in mid sentence and ask, "What's the headline?"

"The headline?" they would ask, stammer, think and . . . leave.

Eventually most everyone solved their own problems. It was easier than trying to think of a headline.

And our friend's day became organized.

HOW MANY SATURDAYS?

Looking at your schedule in a new and different way can determine how you organize your life and your work.

I was once faced with taking on an extra, unrelated-to-our business job. The client offered a good fee but I wasn't excited about the assignment. I tried the Ben Franklin technique, taking a sheet of paper, putting a line down the middle and listing the pros on one side and the cons on the other.

It came out even.

I called our friend and fellow speaker Ray Considine in California and explained the problem and he said, "I have the answer!"

"Great," I said. "What is it?"

"How old are you?" he asked.

"Sixty" I said.

"All right," he answered, you have about 1,000 Saturdays left. How do you want to spend them?"

Only 1,000 Saturdays left in my lifetime? Well, I certainly wouldn't waste them on something I didn't want to do!

THE ANDREW GOH THEORY

We were visiting Dr. John Haggai's Christian Fellowship seminary in Singapore and had a conversation with Andrew Goh, in charge of the youth fellowship program.

We asked how he was able to accomplish so much each day. What was the secret to his organization?

He explained that there were four groups of people in the world:
1. Those who make things happen. That's the smallest group.
2. Those who watch things happen. Next smallest group
3. Those who don't know what's happening. The largest group.
4. Those who don't care if things happen or not.

Andrew called the last group "The Pathetic Apathetic." He said he belonged to the first group because he organized his daily work into specific tasks that had to be done in a specific time. And he kept on checking on himself to make sure he accomplished his goals within the time limits he had set.

TRACY'S LAW OF COMPLEXITY.

I was in a meeting with Brian Tracy, the well-known lecturer on selling and marketing and he said he had devised his "Tracy's Law of Complexity" to help people become better organized. "The technique is simple," said Brian. "The better organized you are, the more in control you are, the less problems and errors you will have."

He said his "Law" proved it.

"Any problem you have becomes more complex the more people you involve. In fact, the complexity of the problem increases by the square of the steps involved."

One person = one chance of error

Two people = four chances of errors

Three people= nine chances of errors

Four people = 16 chances of errors

Five people = 25 chances of errors.

"It keeps on multiplying," says Brian. "The more people or the more steps you have to solve a problem, the more chance for error."

The solution: Organize. Says Brian, "The mark of the superior mind is the ability to hold two contradictory thoughts at the same time and still retain the ability to function."

So if you can solve a problem by yourself, do it!

A related principle is you should **not** do tasks which take time away from your fundamental pursuits.

Example: A friend saw me retyping a manuscript. He said, "How much are you worth an hour?"

"Why?" I asked,

"Well," he said, "I figure a good secretary could type that for you for about $8.00 an hour. Aren't you worth more than that?"

We stopped typing and gave the manuscript to our secretary. The two hours it would take me to retype that column was spent on far more valuable projects.

In Tough Marketing Times, it is vital you spend your time on the most important problems that have to be solved.

H.L. HUNT'S DECISIONS FOR SUCCESS

H. L. Hunt was a Texas oil billionaire who developed four "decisions" for business success:

1. Decide what you want to do.
2. Decide what you'll give up to get it.
3. Decide your priorities.
4. Decide to. . . do it!

These decisions are really **organizational** principals. These simple directions can work for anyone, anywhere in any type of endeavor.

Let's take them one at a time:

1. Decide what you want to do.

In Japan, children start competing a few days after they are born for the best schools. Elementary and high school youngsters go to school during the day and often after dinner as well. They are competing with one another for the availability of slots in college.

In England it is not unusual, a few days after birth, to enroll your son into Eton (or another appropriate school —preferably where the father went. Which was where the grandfather went).

In Switzerland how you score on tests determine not only **if** you will have a higher education but also **what** course you will study.

The above societies may err in being a bit too rigid, a bit too organized too early in life.

But in this country we have the opposite problem. Americans are not sure what they want to do with their life. And, to add sorrow to indecision, are often unhappy with the direction they have chosen. Annual surveys continue to show most Americans are unhappy in their jobs.

Very sad . . .

"But I don't know what I want to do," says the undecided young person or the person making a career change, "and so I can't fulfill the first rule of deciding what-I-want-to-do because I don't know what I want to do!"

Here's one way to try: Eliminate everything you do **not** want to be. Go through common professions: Teacher, doctor, nurse, accountant, attorney, policeman, fireman. And then the not-so-obvious: Environmentalist, archaeologist, zoo keeper. You will soon find you narrow your list rather quickly.

Deciding what you want to do means setting goals.

You must have a plan. You must know where you are going. We want to make sure the pilot in the plane knows where he's going. Or the captain when he's steering the ship. Which is the reason you have maps in your car. And remember — when you cross the goal line of a football field, people cheer.

Set goals and think about them every day in terms of what you are going to do to accomplish them.

Mike Copps, president of Copps supermarkets in Wisconsin, was named head of the United Way in his hometown.

"What's our goal?" he asked.

"An increase of 5.6 percent," he was told.

"Why 5.6 percent?" he asked

"Because it seems right," they answered.

"But," said Mike, "'Does it meet the needs of the community?"

"Oh, no," they said.

"Well, how much do you need?" asked Mike.

"$250,000," they answered, "and that's a 30 percent increase."

"Great!" said Mike. "Let's set a goal of a 40 percent increase."

End of story: They increased their collections that year 172 percent!

Here is another story along the same lines:

I once visited the owner of a men's clothing store and said, "How much more business do you want to do next year, Jeff?"

"Oh about 6 percent," he said. Then he corrected himself. "No, about 9 percent. That will pay for the cost of living and other expenses."

"What would you have to do, Jeff," I asked "to have a 100 percent increase in business?"

"A what?" he said.

"Come on Jeff, you're a businessman. Tell me what would you have to do to double your business?"

He thought for a moment and then said, "Well, we don't need

all the room on the parking lot. We could push the back wall out and put in a small women's clothing shop. We could try some direct mail. We could try staying open nights by appointment. We could . . ."

"Wait a minute," I said, "Are you saying that's it's possible? Are you saying that instead of going ahead 100 percent you only go ahead 60 percent? 40 percent? And a few minutes ago you told me you'd be happy with a 9 percent increase . . ."

David Ogilvy, founder of one of America's most successful advertising agencies, tells of the time when he first started out. He went through magazines and newspapers looking at them and asking the question, "For whom can I do a better job in advertising than is being done now?"

Even though he had just started a small advertising business, he made a list of five major accounts he wanted to acquire:

1. General Foods
2. Bristol Meyers
3. Campbell Soup
4. Lever Brothers
5. Shell Oil

Ogilvy put the five names on a sheet of paper and had them taped on his bathroom mirror. Every morning he would walk into the bathroom and see the five names. And every morning he would ask himself, "What am I going to do **today** to capture one of those five accounts?"

A few years later he had all five!

Why? Because, he said, "That's my goal. That's what I want. And I will work toward achieving that goal."

Mary Robert Rinehart, author of more than fifty novels and one of America's highest paid writers tells how she did it:

"I always thought I could write if I just had the time. But I had three small sons, my husband to look after and my invalid mother. Then, during a financial panic, we lost everything. I was driven frantic by debts. I made up my mind I was going to earn money by writing. So I made a schedule. I planned every hour for the week in advance. And my life took on a new zest."

Jim Volvano, the former coach of the North Carolina State basketball team, tells the story of his father saying to him, "You will be in the NCAA finals and I'm going to be there in my new suit and you're going to win."

That year North Carolina State was eliminated in the first round.

The next year the father repeated his promise and Volvano took the team to the tournament but was eliminated the second round.

The third year the father said, one more time, "You will be in the NCAA finals and I'm going to be there in my new suit and you're going to win."

That year North Carolina State beat Houston for the championship! And his father was there in his new suit.

Three weeks later Volvano get a phone call. His father died at 1:30 in the morning. He had a heart attack.

Moral: If you have someone who believes in you, you can do anything!

Why use fifty words when five will do?

We tend to take too much time to do a job. Or use too many words to tell a story. Writers often ramble and use twenty words when three will do the job. And often better.

Direct mail writers say letters become more more effective when the writer throws away the first two paragraphs he has written.

Abraham Lincoln made one of the most famous speeches ever given. The man who preceded him to the platform spoke for two hours. Lincoln spoke for two minutes. The photographers did not have a chance to set up their equipment!

No one remembers what speaker Edward Everett said. But Lincoln's Gettysburg address will live forever. Everett wrote his thoughts in a note to Lincoln the next day: "I should be glad if I could flatter myself that I came as near to the central idea of the occasion in two hours as you did in two minutes."

Quantity of words does not indicate quality of thought. Genesis tells the creation of the world in 442 words.

The Bible needs only 118 words to convey 62 percent of its meaning.

The Reverend J. Knoles of London listed the first 100,000 words in the Bible and found that 118 simple words are used so often they make up 62,456 of the first 100,000 words. In other words, a child or foreigner who knew only these 118 words could still read 62 percent of the text of the bible.

There are more than 500,000 words in the English language. But the spoken language of the streets is so limited that anyone familiar with 200 or 300 commonly used words can understand 90 percent of everything that is said in ordinary conversation — and make a good guess at the remaining 10 percent.

This does not mean you do things quickly just for the sake of doing them quickly. Quality cannot be rushed.

The pianist Leopold Godowski had a tailor make him a suit for a national tour. The tailor kept on postponing the day for finishing the suit. Exasperated, Godowski said to the tailor, "You know it's taking you six weeks for a pair of pants. It only took God six days to create the universe."

"So," said the tailor, "look at it!"

2. Decide what you'll give up to get it.

You mean I have to work more than 40 hours?

You mean I have to give up Saturdays on my boat?

You mean I have to get up at 6 in the morning to get that done?

Achieving success means making sacrifices. And when you succeed, people will wonder how it all happened.

A famous actor tells of the time a fan approached and said, "Wow, you make all that money and do all the traveling. You're really lucky. "

And he answered, "Yes, it only took me twenty five years to be an overnight success."

Weight Watchers tells you to list all the items you eat during the day. And you are amazed when you see it all written down. Why not list what-you-do every hour of the day for a week. And you will be amazed at the time you spend doing little. Or nothing.

We had a friend Tom who was a lawyer. Very busy. We once asked him, "What would you like to do, Tom if you had the time?"

"Read. I used to read almost a novel a week in college. But you can see how busy I am. Taking home this thick briefcase every night. No time to myself."

"Could you give me 15 minutes tomorrow, Tom, if I call you?" we asked.

"Sure," he said.

"How about 15 minutes every day for the rest of the year?"

"Are you kidding? Do you know how busy I am? I won't even get through half the papers in this briefcase tonight."

"Come on, Tom. Fifteen minutes a day. That's not much. Set your alarm clock 15 minutes earlier. Take your phone off the hook at lunch time. you can do it."

"Oh well," he said,"that's what friends are for. You got it!"

"Terrific," we answered. "Now say, 'Thank you.'"

"What for?" he asked.

"Because we just gave you eleven days to read next year!"

"What?"

"Take out that computer you always carry in that briefcase of yours. Add it up. 15 minutes a day for 350 days a year equals eleven 8 hour days. And you said you didn't have the time . . ."

What that story proves: We **do** have the time. We tend to simply follow Parkinson's Law that work expands to fit the time allotted. If we have an hour to do a job, it takes an hour. If we have fifteen minutes to do the same job, we find we can accomplish it in fifteen minutes!

3. Decide your priorities.

Henry L. Doherty, the great industrialist, said, "I can hire men to do everything but two things: Think and do things in the order of their importance."

Each day has 24 hours and 1,440 minutes. Doing what has to be done first increases your chance for success. Start by drawing up a list of priorities. Next to it put the approximate time required to do the job.

Now, what happens if the first job is difficult? Or takes too long? Or is unpleasant? You decide you'll come back to it later. Let's start with number five. That's easy.

The problem with that solution is you wind up doing the less important jobs which may turn out to be so much wasted effort because the important job (That's number one. See it up there. Top of the list. Still there.) was never done.

Go back to job number one.Break it down into time segments. Every job has several parts. By completing the parts, you will soon finish the job.

4. Decide ... to do it!

Russell Gohn of Philadelphia Life Insurance Company said that when he hears other salesman complain about business and say it is because of (check one) the weather, the economy, the competition, the time of the year, he answers, "Well, it's nothing that 2,000 interviews won't cure."

Decide your priorities. Then get to work.

WHAT HAPPENED AFTER THE MUTINY

Captain William Bligh of the HMS Bounty is remembered by most of us from the movie, "Mutiny on the Bounty." We remember the superb performance of Charles Laughton in the original movie version. We recall his arrogance and pomposity, an altogether evil man. Recent evidence tells us this picture might well be exaggerated. The authors Charles Nordhoff and James Hall in their novel, "Men Against The Seas," showed another and more favorable side to Bligh.

Let us examine who he was. And what happened after the mutiny.

Bligh was trained by Captain Cook, the famous explorer and navigator who discovered the Hawaiian Islands and Australia. Bligh was the first British seaman promoted through the ranks to captain.

The Bounty was his first ship. His crew had a handful of qualified seamen. Most were murderers and thieves from British "gaols" who choose the sea in preference to the hangman's noose.

Fletcher Christian was **not** the first mate (contrary to the movie rendition) but a **third** mate.

On April 28, 1789, Bligh was cast out by the mutineers into a small open long boat. Only 18 of his men (nearly half the 44 man crew) joined him in what was thought by all to be eventual death.

Now, let us examine how Bligh organized his crew using H.L. Hunt's rules of decisions as a framework.

1. Decide what you want to do: Bligh decided he would lead his crew to safety. He asked each man to take his hand and pledge their acceptance to him as captain.

He taught the men to survive: Wringing out shirts in water to put on their heads to prevent heat stroke.

2. Decide what you'll give up to get it: Bligh punished himself unmercifully. He lashed himself to the tiller. The men knew he was there.They could count on him. He was visible. He was confident.

3. Decide your priorities: Bligh studied the winds and waters. He found small islands to stop at to renew food and water supplies. He lost only one man who was speared by natives. When the sun shone he spent his time charting the waters with writing material wrapped in oil skins under his seat. He constantly exuded optimism and enthusiasm. He told his men he would bring them back safely.

4. Decide to . . . do it!: His journey lasted 46 days and covered 4,000 miles!

When at last Bligh and his crew sailed into the Port of Timor in the East Indies, all the men were in rags. All the men were unconscious. Except Bligh. He brought the boat into the harbor at early dawn. A child ran down to the dock curious to see this strange vessel and equally strange cargo. Bligh did not untie the ropes lashing him to the tiller. He looked at the young boy and said, "Go quickly and fetch the Governor of this island."

The Governor arrived and untied Bligh's ropes. Bligh staggered to his feet and saluted the Governor saying, "Permission to come ashore, Sir." And collapsed.

But he did it. He did it through organization.

IS IT ANYBODY'S JOB?

This is a story about four people:
Everybody, Somebody, Anybody and Nobody.
There was an important job to be done and
Everybody was asked to do it.
Everybody was sure Somebody would do it.
Anybody could have done it, but Nobody did it.
Somebody got angry about that because it was
Everybody's job.
Everybody thought Anybody could do it, but
Nobody realized that
Everybody wouldn't do it. It ended up that
Everybody blamed Somebody when actually
Nobody asked Anybody.

TOM HAGGAI INTRODUCTION

Tom Haggai became a Baptist preacher at the age of 15. In the more than four decades since then, Tom has touched the lives of thousands of people with his message of faith and hard work.

But in order to accomplish all his goals, Tom has to be extremely organized. Consider some of his ongoing work:

- Speaking to hundreds of organizations around the world;
- Putting together a radio broadcast heard throughout the country;
- Heading up the THA Foundation, which provides college scholarships to deserving youngsters;
- Serving on numerous corporate boards,
- And, by the way, working as Chairman of the Board and CEO of IGA stores, one of the largest retail grocery chains in the country.

Tom became head of IGA in a roundabout way. IGA was struggling about 15 years ago, and Tom was invited in as a motivational speaker. The Board was so taken with his speech that they invited him to serve on the Board. After several years in that capacity, he was recruited to run the organization.

In the interview that follows, Tom shows how he is organizing IGA to be a worldwide power in the food industry. But this introduction to Tom Haggai would not be complete unless I shared a personal story about my relationship with Tom.

A TOM HAGGAI STORY

I had just lost $406,000.

It started out at an enthusiastic meeting with a group of local businessmen. Casinos had just arrived in Atlantic City and we were excited about the new opportunities. Why not open a television station? We would soon be on the map of the world as a new tourist destination. Certainly a TV station would be successful.

Everyone contributed $5,000 and thought it was a sure thing. It was not.

Despite the initial enthusiasm, progress was slow. And

expensive. Soon we found ourselves signing one bank note after another promising to pay back loans that were reaching astronomical peaks. And soon, the TV station failed.

Like all successes and failures there is never one reason — usually a series of reasons. Ours included interest rates jumping to more than 20 percent, too much money spent on the studios, a poor choice as station manager, a succession of unsuccessful sales manager . . .

The station went bankrupt. An outstanding friend and lawyer was able to hold our personal losses to only $406,000. Only $406,000!!!

Over 25 years ago, our family had developed a shopping center in Atlantic City, New Jersey. Starting with a tiny children's shop, it soon grew into nearly a city block in size. What I learned to do (and not to do) I put into books, columns and seminars. I was just beginning to achieve success in this new motivation business when the bill for the failed TV station came due.

With all my resources and income, I was still short $2,000 a month! Where would this money come from?

My usually optimistic mood became dreary. I became consumed with the inability to raise an extra $2,000 a month. I told some close friends about my problem and they all told me not to become obsessed. I called friend and mentor Tom Haggai in his home and talked for an hour and he reassured me and said I had the ability and talent and I should persevere.

I knew there was a solution out there.

But where?

Then, one day, I received a phone call from Tom Haggai. He said he wanted me to meet him in a distant city. I was to fly there the following Monday and return home the same day.

Was I to give a speech? What was the reason for the trip?

No speech. No reason. Just be there.

I arrived, was met by Tom, and we drove to see the CEO of a major corporation. Obviously the meeting had been arranged by Tom. The CEO talked about his plans for the future and wanted me involved to consult and do programs for the small businesses that belonged to his giant conglomerate. He suggested a monthly retainer for my services.

(Yes, the exact same amount need to pay back our debt to the bank.)

We accepted graciously and through the years did programs, seminars and consulting for this great company.

After the meeting, Tom took us back to the airport and we were unable to talk, completely caught up in the emotion of the moment.

He left me off at the departure gate and I quietly asked, trying to keep myself under control, "How can I ever pay you back?" He smiled, and waved goodbye.

I remember standing at the airport, watching his car go away, feeling the tears of gratitude and then, suddenly, his car backed up. The window rolled down. Tom looked at me and said, "I just thought how you can pay me back."

"How?" I asked. "Anything. Name it."

He looked at me and quietly said, "Help someone else . . . "

TOM HAGGAI INTERVIEW
Q. How do American business fight out of a recession?

A.   There is a rule of thumb I use: You economize for efficiency, but you sell for prosperity. I've always had people much older than I as advisors. Without exception they told me they made their best business decisions in tough times. Not their best profits, but their best decisions. And they never let tough times keep them from having a strategy for progress.

We've had businesses lately that have been run from quarter to quarter because they have been controlled by stock analysts rather than CEOs. The heads of business have been CEOs in title only. They have allowed the control of their business to be moved over to Wall Street. The have allowed big hunks of stock to be held in the hands of institutions and institutional managers who are only concerned about short-term profits. If I'm managing a teachers union portfolio, all I care about is whether XYZ company produces a 20 percent return for me. Therefore, many CEOs today are not managing their business and because of that they are in a very vulnerable position when times get tough.

Q. *Is one of the things required for success of American businesses that the people running it should have a stake in the company?*

A. Yes, and they should also have long term desire to stay there. The very top management has been somewhat isolated. When you say a company is cutting out two hundred key positions, that very seldom includes an executive vice president. It still might be a vice president but it is essentially middle management, directors and managers of departments. I think people who are going to turn their companies around are people who don't have to respond quarter by quarter.

Q. *Translating that in to what your doing with IGA, is one of the reasons you're expanding globally because you have a long term outlook?*
A. One of the big problems I have is the board members who say that we have so much to do in the U.S., we don't need you traveling. That is a very short term outlook. Foreign countries have come seeking us, but I wasn't hard to persuade because we needed something to energize ourselves internally.

I see overseas expansion as a long-term chance to grow. We are over food stored in the U.S., by anybody's definition. We had to have some new frontiers for IGA to grow. The frontiers don't stop in California. They stop wherever the world is until they meet themselves coming from east to west. There is nothing new about overseas expansion because J. Frank Grimes who founded IGA had a global outlook.

Q. *What are the advantage to foreign and domestic supermarkets joining forces?*

A. Domestic retailers are excited. Now they think they're are part of something worldwide. When you have a license to franchise, it is important your franchisee has a positive mind set. And our overseas stores who become IGA members enjoy at least a 20 percent increase in their business with our system put in place. And that is the low side. Most of them are experiencing increases around 25 percent and some have increased over 30 percent. We are bringing them a system that they needed.

Q. *What is this system? Is it technology?*

A. It's shelving, it's store control, product control, inventory control, store styling, services rendered to the customer, advertising, public relations, even such things as Special Olympics (*Editor's note: IGA is a leading corporate contributor to Special Olympics*). In fact the new IGA company in western Australia that just joined us had a million dollar dinner, the largest Special Olympics dinner ever held.

Q. *What are the foreign supermarkets giving to IGA in addition to franchise fees?*

A. Soon there will be worldwide buying of food products and we see our relationship with foreign supermarkets as a sourcing alliance which can be very valuable. Look at the drought in California. It is in the third year. If it goes on we have to start looking for some other sources for produce. Our foreign partners are currently sourcing other places. We also see it as a tremendous alliance when it comes to non-food products such as toys, tools, chairs and tables. Those are items where the food store makes a larger margin.

Q. *Is selling non-food items a growing trend at IGA establishments?*

A. We push it because non-foods is one of the few areas where our stores are going to make any money. They are not going to make any money in the center of the store on the real things that we think of as a food store. They don't make any money on the canned goods. They do make money on produce, meat, dairy and deli. Non-foods becomes another level of excellent profits. There is a much better profit margin in non-foods than in other areas of the supermarket.

The Wal-mart and K-marts are going to put food in their stores They are doing more and more of it. My idea is that the food store have the same amount of non-food products as the discount stores have food products. Just reverse the percentage. A Wal-mart might have 10 to 15 percent food products. We would have 10 to 15 percent general merchandise.

Q. One of the exciting themes in recent years for the IGA stores in America was the slogan "Hometown Proud." Can you give me some idea of the campaign's genesis?

A. We won a number of awards for that campaign. Before we created "Hometown Proud," we had presentations by a number of national advertising firms, and they were good. But we are different than the typical national account. We don't make our big money in some of the major cities. We are in Minneapolis and Cincinnati. But we are not in New York City and we're not in Chicago and the advertising firms had trouble designing a national approach which didn't include those major cities.

After thinking about our advertising approach, I focused on two concepts.

First, it dawned on me that on our board we have five of the top seven food wholesale companies in America and the seventeen food wholesale companies on our board represent 51 percent of the non-chain store supermarket business. Many of the companies on our board have a vice-president who is as talented in advertising as anybody at a public advertising company.

I realized that what we usually get from advertising firms is one senior person, one journeyman and one person that has just received his degree from college in advertising. We can bring into our boardroom five men whose career depends on their success in advertising food companies. So I decided to have our board become involved with creating a new image for IGA.

The second thing I realized was that we had to change our image. We were saying to our customers you should shop at our stores because we grew up together and we went to school together. We had to get rid of that kind of thinking. Nobody owes us a thing. We owe our customers a good place to shop, not the cheapest necessarily, but a shopping "experience." So we had to say, "We are here to serve you. We hope you like us. We are going to be a good place for you to shop."

Our board worked on our image and came up with "Hometown Proud." The idea is: We're proud of our town. We're proud to be located here. We thank you for letting us have our store here. We're going to serve you. We're going to take part in the community. We're going to support little league ball. We're going to support scouting, etc. We hope that you also find this a pleasant place to shop. We're going to start with the premise that we are a community citizen, we care about the community.

Because we care we are going to try to have a store that tries to show how much we care. It is going to be pleasant and bright, good place to sit around. We'll have someone who carries your groceries out. We will be a caring place. Whether you shop with us or not we're going to care about this town. We're not going to think that you owe us this business. We're going to earn your business and we thank you for letting us be here.

Q. Before you had the Hometown Proud brand image, was there anything that identified IGA stores other than the label IGA?

A. No, it was pretty much by region, sections and just whim and wish. We did not have a national blanket. We now have over ninety percent of our stores who in their annual reports to us say they are using Hometown Proud.

Q. Are you trying to encourage IGA stores to be bigger?

A. It cannot be reduced to simply big or small. A big store that is dirty and unkempt is guilty of small thinking. I am more concerned with big thinking. We are in 48 states within the U.S. and we have many overseas stores. We want our stores to be sizable enough to be a major factor in their communities. In western Nebraska and Kansas a store of 12,000 square feet may be as big as that town needs. If that town is near a big city, it might have to be bigger than that. When you have a store that is 40 miles from the next town and this town is a town of 6,000 people out in the prairie, then that store would not have to be so big. But it has to have all of the departments in it, and it has to be fresh and clean and sharp looking.

It is not size alone that counts. But, in general, we are looking to attract bigger stores. In Hartsville, Ohio, a town of 2,500 people, we have a 52,000 square foot store. It had to be because it is right next to Akron. In Millersberg, Ohio we just opened a store of 52,500 square feet in a town of 18,000.

In 1990 we opened a new store every 36 hours. That has not been done by any chain or voluntary group since the 1930's. Our new stores average better than 17,000 square feet, which is fifty percent larger than the old stores. We went up to over a billion dollar in sales last year. We had an increase of 15 percent in total sales last year, which is as good as the best.

Q. What are the ingredients that have made your organization thrive even though we are in this recession and times are tough?

A. Recession always brings back tradition. When things tighten up, we go back to what we think we can trust and that is tradition. Therefore, when people want to give us credit we don't take credit. We're just the right format in the right place. We have sitting areas in our store for people just to visit and have a cup of coffee on us. We may have a branch of the post office or drive-in windows or home deliveries in our stores. Those are the things that America needs as we go back to a traditional approach.

Q. Your background is in teaching and ministry. What would you say to college graduates today or people starting out who feel that this is going to be a tough time?

A. Early on, they need to know whether they want to work for someone else or if they want to work for themselves. There are people that would be totally insecure with their own business. They need to work for a large corporation. I admire them for that and I would say to them be the best manager, best director and try to work your way to the top.

But there are many people that want their own business. It is still possible to do it. There is a store in one of our towns that cost 2.5 million dollars when it was finished. It was a beautiful brand new store and the couple who runs it mortgaged everything and finally came up with $60,000 and we put them in business with that and they are doing mighty well. They couldn't go in to a fast food restaurant with $60,000. We would have put them in for less than that.

We have another store that the couple went in with $6,000. The store is worth about $2 million. We believe it is important to qualify the people in our organization.

Q. How did you get started to try to make the best you possibly could of yourself?

A. My parents. I had achieving parents. My mom was so quiet. There was a lady who was supposed to die at my birth, or we both could have. She lived to be eighty and never had a healthy day in her life and yet when she died I never could remember hearing my mother complain. She just didn't. The nearest she came to complaining was when she was in the hospital near her death and I asked her how she was doing. She said, "I just think that they are feeding me too well and it is more than I can eat." That was the way she complained.

On the other side I had this Lebanese father who was driven and he helped me. He balanced Mom. The only way I knew that I wasn't doing anything bad was that he wasn't complaining. He was short on praise and quick on criticism. He believed that doing a good job should not be praised. It should be expected. I don't quite buy that. I hit the middle on that. Mom might have been too complimentary, but dad did not believe that you should be rewarded for doing your job. The job should be done because you said that you would do it.

My dad learned English perfectly and he even taught English. We went without food so we could by books for the library, which he thought was a worthy sacrifice to be an effective minister. His pet line to me was, "Whatever you do, do it well. You never know when God is in the shadows measuring you for bigger opportunity." As Stanley Marcus said, "There is no job so small that you can afford to overlook it, or any challenge so large that you should be afraid to face it."

Q. How about the business articles that say the country is doing badly and economic times are hard?

A. I reject those. I believe that people that do well have faith in this country. They know that one of the reasons people invest in the U.S. is that we have a stable government. They have faith in their family and the company that they are heading, the product they are producing. The money they make is just a way of keeping score.

COMPETE!

COMPETE! INTRODUCTION

Americans love to compete. From the World Series to the Miss America Pageant to spelling bees to chili cookoffs, Americans love to vie to be the best.

Successful businesspeople have the same zeal for succeeding in business that they have for succeeding in weekend sports contests. They view business as a sophisticated game, and they try to use strategy and hard work to come away with the grand prize — business success. This chapter shows how successful businesspeople are driven to compete — and succeed.

COMPETE! QUOTES

Famous football coach **Bear Bryant** once went duck hunting. He shot at one duck and it kept on flying. He turned to his friend and said, "Now there flies a dead duck."

"When economic times get tough, one of the mistakes we make as retailers and vendors is to start playing it safe. Once you do that there really is **no** reason for the customer to buy." — **Michael Sullivan**, CEO Merry-Go-Round Enterprises.

"Make no little plans. They have no magic to stir men's blood and probably themselves will not be realized. Make big plans; aim high in hope and work, remembering that a noble, logical diagram once recorded will never die, but long after we are gone will be a living thing, asserting itself with evergrowing insistency. Let your watchword be order and your beacon beauty." — **Daniel H. Burnham**

"The American system of ours, call it Americanism, call it capitalism, call it what you like, gives each and every one of us a great opportunity if we only seize it with both hands and make the most of it." — **Al Capone.**

THE TEXAS RANGER

One day, in the early 1900s, a mayor in a town bordering Mexico was having a problem. Some of the Mexicans and Texans were involved in a fight that spread the brawl to an uncontrollable slug fest. The mayor called the nearest Ranger station and said, "Quick. Send the Rangers. We're having a riot!"

Soon, the Mayor saw a cloud of dust in the distance. He ran to the edge of town to greet the rescue team. As the dust cleared, he saw only one rider and one horse. The Ranger dismounted and the Mayor asked in exasperation, "Hey! Where is everybody else?"

And the Ranger looked at the mayor and calmly replied: "One riot. One Ranger."

Now, **that's** confidence.

COMPETE! TECHNIQUES

1. I know something about the person I'm trying to sell before I try to make the sale.

If I'm going to someone's office, I read information about that person ahead of time. Their likes, dislikes, school they went to, marital status.

If that's not possible, I look around their office while I'm waiting. What awards and diplomas are on the walls? What kind of pictures are on the desk? Start the conversation off in terms of his or her interests, **not yours.** Soon you will find the conversation flowing easily.

In my store I find a person's occupation and ask something about their job. I talk about almost anything **except** the merchandise.

2. I am quick to admit mistakes or say, "Sorry, I was wrong about that." This comes **only** with self-confidence. You know your store, your business. Your personal ego has been built through the years and prospered because you are good. No one is right every time. If you are quick to say, "I was wrong about that," you'll be amazed how fast the customer switches to **your** side.

One time a man bought ten shirts from us. They were expensive: $50 each. One of his arms was slightly shorter than the other. He asked if we would shorten the one sleeve for him. We said, "Sure. But let's try just one shirt to make sure it comes out OK."

Our tailor shortened the one shirt and it fit perfectly. We then did the other nine and gave them to the customer.

He returned to the store the next day very upset. For some reason the altered sleeves were all too short. The salesperson wasn't really listening to the complaint. He saw $450 worth of damaged shirts we could never use. He tried reasoning, blaming the tailor, all to no avail. The customer yelled louder and stronger. My salesman called on me to help.

I came down from my office and saw a furious customer. Through the years I had learned the first step to handling an irate customer is to simply let them talk. And so I said, "Would you mind taking the time to tell me the problem?" He did! And ended with wanting to know, "what you're going to do about his stupid mistake!"

Let an angry customer speak until he is through. Don't interrupt. They have to say what they have to say.

Talk in a quiet, low voice. This is in direct contrast to the high, loud voice used by the customer. Now he has to listen carefully to what you are saying.

When he finished, I quietly said, "Can I ask you a question? Please tell me why you even bothered to come back to this store?"

"**What?**" he yelled.

"I have to tell you," I said, "that I would be angry if I was treated the way you have been treated — shirts all botched up, having to explain why you brought them back. Why, that's terrible. I'd never shop here again."

He stopped, looked at me quizzically. I continued.

"I want you to know something right now," I said. "All you have to do is to tell me what will make you happy and you've got it. You are not allowed to walk through the front door of this store and have bad feelings about us. We won't permit that. Just tell me what you want, and I'll say 'Yes'."

He looked at me, not sure he heard what I was saying.

"Now, be careful," I continued, "because whatever you want, I'm going to give to you. So think about it first. You can have new shirts. You can have your money back. Whatever you want . . ."

"Well, he said, now quiet. "I don't want my money back. I want shirts."

"OK" I said, "you have nine new shirts today. Now, here's another idea. How about if I take the shirts that don't fit and make short sleeves out of them. That way you'll have an **extra** nine shirts to use this summer."

Now remember, like most retailers, we keystone our prices. That means the $50 shirts cost us $25. So when I gave him **another** nine shirts, I was breaking even.

Yes, it cost me a few dollars for tailoring. But what is a few dollars compared to a lost customer?

"You're going to give me nine new shirts? And then you're going to fix all the others into short sleeves and give those to me as well?"

"Yes," I answered, "and now will you do me a favor?"

"Sure," he said, "what do you want?"

"I want to make sure the new shirts fit perfectly so would you take them to *your* tailor and have him shorten them for you?" (I didn't want **another** nine shirts coming back on a difficult alteration.)

By this time we were friends and he agreed.

As he left with his nine new shirts, we insisted he take a $30 silk tie to pay for his expenses driving back and forth to the store for what was our fault.

Within the year, this person was responsible for more than $5,000 in sales in our store between personal purchases and customers he brought to the store that, as he told his friends, "They won't let you leave until you're happy."

3. I honestly believe what I am selling will be of value to the customer. Not just any merchandise I have in stock but merchandise I feel is right for that customer. It must "fit" them.

In insurance, it is policies that fit my customer's income and family size.

In automobiles, it is a car that fits my customer's personality.

In real estate, a house that fits my customer's life style.

In clothing, it is the right color, the right style and the right "fit."

I cannot just sell products. They must be products that fit my customer. And I have to convince myself before I can convince my customer.

4. I'm reluctant to suggest new projects I don't have time for.
One of the greatest reasons for failure is not the collapse of a project but the collapse of follow-through. When I attend meetings for my city, county or state I am very careful what I volunteer to do or even suggest because someone will say, "Why don't you handle that?"

That one question, if I agree to it, usually involves dozens or hundreds of hours.

I have to be careful what I say "Yes" to because I feel the responsibility to follow through. I find a commitment, once accepted, means another rejected. So having self confidence also means saying "No" to some work opportunities.

SELF CONFIDENCE MEANS A BURNING DESIRE TO WIN

Ty Boyd, a great speaker, tells of the time he met tennis champion Martina Navratilova and asked her why she was such a consistent champion. She told him, "Because I hate to lose."

Self confidence was never a problem with Leroy Robert Satchel Paige, one of the legends in baseball.

All through his peak years, blacks were barred from the major leagues. Of his 2,500 games, more than 2,000 were with black ball clubs in black leagues. Advance billboards would read: **"Greatest Pitcher, Guaranteed To Strike Out The First Nine Men."** And he did.

His self confidence was legendary. Here are two of his typical routines:

1. He would point to one of the infielders. With the next pitch the batter grounded out to **that** infielder. Before the next pitch, he pointed to another infielder. And the next batter grounded out to

the man Satchel indicated. For the third out, he would point to himself. And strike out the last man!

(People still refer to Babe Ruth pointing to the field where he would hit the next ball out of the park. And that was just **one** pitch in **one** game!)

2. Paige would suddenly stop the game and wave the outfielders off the field. Then he would face the next three batters and they would ground out — or strike out!

Entrepreneur Bill Veeck brought Paige to his team, the Cleveland Indians, in 1948 where he drew great crowds.

In 1965, approaching 65, he pitched a full inning and retired three batters in a row.

He made the baseball Hall of Fame in 1971.

SELF CONFIDENCE IS DOING FOR OTHERS

If you like, approve, respect someone, they seem to like, admire and respect you as well. Just a small variation of the Golden Rule. (Conversely: If you dislike, disapprove, or disrespect someone they tend to dislike, disapprove and disrespect you as well).

David Dunn in his book, **"Try Giving Yourself Away,"** writes dozens of ideas you can do every day to make someone else's life a little better. A note, a gesture, a phrase of praise. That's really all it takes. It was Lord Chesterfield in one of his famous letters to his son who wrote, "My son, here is the way to have people like you: Make every person like himself a little better and I promise that he or she will like you better, too."

And you have to do it yourself. Self confidence is **not** inherited. No matter how famous and sure-about-themselves your parents were. As the Irish say, "You've got to do your own growing, no matter how tall your grandfather was."

SELF CONFIDENCE IS BELIEF IN YOUR DREAM

When the automobile first arrived, Literary Digest wrote, "The ordinary 'horseless carriage' is a luxury for the wealthy. It will never, of course, come into common use like the bicycle." But Henry Ford had a dream and made it come true.

Simon Newcomb wrote at the beginning of this century, "Flight by machines heavier than air is unpractical and insignificant if not utterly impossible." But the Wright Brothers went to Kitty Hawk in 1903 and made their dream come true.

The British Parliament sent an investigator to observe Edison's incandescent lamp. His report: "The idea is good enough for our trans-Atlantic friends, but unworthy of the attention of practical or scientific men."

And even brilliant people have blind spots.

Naysayers include:

H. G. Wells, writing about submarines: "I must confess my imagination refuses to see any use of a submarine doing anything but suffocating its crew and floundering at sea."

D. W. Griffith, the giant of the silent movies: "Speaking movies are impossible. When a century has passed, all thought of our so-called 'speaking movies' will have been abandoned. It will never be possible to synchronize the voice with the picture."

But, on the side of the dreamers: Martin Luther King writes a powerful statement and creates a movement from a Birmingham jail. Anne Frank leaves an indelible memory in a diary written while she is hiding from the Nazis in the top floor of an Amsterdam home.

Their attitude was always positive. They never ceased to believe.

WHATEVER HAPPENED TO THE HERBIE BERGERS?

One of the first salesmen we had call on us in our retail store was Herbie Berger. He would visit us twice a year in his Cadillac which he traded in every year. His clothing was immaculate: three piece vested suit, shined shoes, proper coat and hat. He could easily have been mistaken for a Wall Street trader. But he was actually the prototype "drummer" — the Salesman of Salesmen.

He would always call for an appointment. Then he would arrive, greet everyone and first tell us (not show us) what great merchandise we would see that day. At just the right moment he gestured to his trainee who would set up the floor rack and hang the giant cloth garment bags. Herb would reach inside the bag, much like a magician into the top hat for the first pigeon. As each piece was taken out, Herb explained the colors and fabrics available. It was show time! He was supremely confident in what he had and what he **knew** he would sell us that day.

He never walked out without an order larger than the previous season.

He never doubted he would.

We once asked when he developed this self confidence.

"From the time I started," he said, "I could **not** afford the clothes or the car. And so I went to the bank and borrowed money. My parents signed the note. I used the money for clothes and my first Cadillac (yes, my parents signed for the car too). I knew that I could not make the first sale in the first store unless I had the confidence in myself and showed that confidence to the customer."

SELF CONFIDENCE IS HAVING A FIRST CLASS ATTITUDE

Think about it. Who wants to be a second class person doing a second class job?

People work, function and perform first class because of how they believe, no matter where they are. Which brings us to our last story and how traveling First Class is a basic ingredient of Self Confidence.

The year is 1926. The place is Kansas City, Missouri. A young artist named Walt Disney has just gone bankrupt. His attempt to put together a new idea called animation in movies failed in his home town of Kansas City. He decided to go to Hollywood because that's where the future of the movie industry was located.

He never finished high school. His one ambition was to draw and his only art training consisted of a few Saturday morning classes at the local museum.

Now he needed money for a train ticket because in 1926, that is how you went to Los Angeles from Kansas City, Missouri — by train.

He had a camera and took pictures of babies which he sold. But he still did not have enough money. And so he sold the camera to have enough for the ticket he wanted.

And he boarded the train in Kansas City, Missouri wearing a plaid sport jacket and mismatched plaid pants and carrying a cardboard suitcase with three changes of underwear. And he rode the train in the **First Class** compartment!

"I wanted to arrive in Hollywood First Class," he said, "I wanted to feel good about myself. Because I only know how to do things in a first class manner."

And those who have seen his films and the Disney parks know that was his philosophy. The philosophy of a man constantly surrounded by overwhelming debt but cared not. Simply because he knew he would do what he wanted to do.

Why not? **He was Self Confident.**

TOOTING YOUR OWN HORN

The idea is to find that which makes you different than the competition — whatever the competition is. We call this philosophy of self-promotion "Tooting Your Own Horn." The self-promotion is not egotistical. You just want everyone to find out what is unique about your company.

Side note: The competition is not just someone who carries the same or similar merchandise as you. The competition is anyone who says to consumers when they receive their weekly pay check, "Hey, spend some of that money with me. It's more important to buy my (choose one: car, shirt, insurance policy, CD, stereo, TV, widget) than to buy their (same items)."

Finding out what makes you different and makes people want to come to buy from you is what famed advertising man Rosser Reeves called USP. It stands for Unique Selling Proposition. Like its first cousin, ESP (Extra Sensory Perception) it gives you the competitive edge.

Each of you reading this book has some unique characteristic or ability that makes you and your business different from everyone else. The problem is you have lived so long with that unique characteristic that you no longer recognize it as unique. You think everyone else has the same ability/talent. Not true.

I once did advertising for an Ethan Allen furniture store. Looking for something that made him different from all other furniture stores, I had the owner take me through his warehouse. I noticed two carpenters working on furniture.

"What's that?" I asked.

"Oh, we guarantee all Ethan Allen wooden furniture for the buyer's lifetime," said the owner of the store. "If anyone ever has a problem, they bring it back to us and we'll fix it for for them free."

"Wow," we said, "that's terrific. How do you let the world know you do this?"

"Oh" he said, truly believing his words, "Everyone knows we do that."

"Really?" we replied. And put together a series of ads headlined: **"When you buy Ethan Allen wooden furniture we guarantee every piece of furniture will last your lifetime!"**

Sales doubled. Obviously "everyone" did not know he had this service.

If you are an accomplished whittler, harmonica player, pastry-maker, home fixer-upper, you are tempted to believe everyone can do what you can do. Surprise! They cannot. You can take these individual talents that are yours alone and use them in your business.

If your store has free gift wrapping, free mailing, free alterations, free whatever, tell your customer again and again and again. Don't fall into the Curse of Assumption. Simply because **you** know it's there, everyone else must know as well, right? Wrong. You have to tell your customers over and over again what you do that makes you "different." Otherwise the customer thinks all supermarkets are alike because they all sell food. And all insurance agents are alike because they all sell life insurance. And all clothing stores are alike because they all sell clothing. And all banks are alike because they all sell financial services. And . . .

well, you get the idea. Within each person, within each business there exists a particular idiosyncracy that is yours alone - your own individual USP. Seek it out. Flaunt it. To successfully *compete!*

HOW IT WORKED FOR OUR BUSINESS:

I was doing a marketing seminar in Helsinki, Finland and noticed a large crowd at the Intercontinental Hotel. I asked the concierge what was happening and he said, "This is the time of Vateva, our annual fashion fair for winter clothing for next year."

Next year? This was January and they were showing items for next year already?

We quickly learned that Finland was the first European country to offer clothing to buyers for the **following** winter. They had the first scheduled fashion fair in Europe. It was like New Hampshire being first in the Presidential primaries. With one big, big exception. **Everyone** did not go there to see the show. Only the European countries. No one from America. Since we owned several clothing stores in our retail complex, we decided to see the show.

We were amazed. For the first time we saw bright colors in outerwear. Splashes of designs and patterns and stripes. Outerware available in the U.S. at that time contained only solid, dull colors.

We asked if any U.S. stores carried this stunning ski clothing. Most of the companies told us they could not sell U.S. stores.

Why not? Well, the orders from the department stores would be so huge their factories could not handle the production for major U.S. chains and also supply their own customers in Scandinavia, France, Germany.

But what if we wanted to buy just a few hundred? That would be fine.

There we were, in Helsinki, Finland at the major fashion fair and there were no other American buyers!

We placed orders for men's, women's and children's ski jackets.

When they arrivied in August we promoted our "Exclusive In The U.S. Finnish Ski Jackets."

We romanced them. We advertised them. We did direct mail pieces on them. One by one customers came, bought and soon we sold out. We had underestimated the power of the merchandise. And it was too late to re-order!

The following year we bought **three times** as many jackets. We pre-addressed postcards and sent them from Finland to our top 500 customers telling them we were buying exclusive Finnish jackets just for them.

When we returned home in February, the calls started: "When will my jacket arrive?" "Don't forget to call me as soon as they come to the store."

That year we again sold every jacket!

The following year we discontinued buying outerwear from anyone else. We became known as the "store where they have those Finnish jackets."

For several years, this merchandise paid our bills and returned a nice profit.

What had we done? Separated ourselves from all other stores that sold winter jackets not just in our home town, our state, but the country! Within a few years we were shipping Finnish jackets to different states for customers who came to Atlantic City on vacation one year, found the jackets and placed standing orders to mail them when they arrived.

We found our own unique USP in outerwear. All clothing stores were **not** alike. We were the ones with the Finnish jackets.

Years later, other stores began to carry the jackets as well. **But,** we were the first! We established the beachhead. We built the relationships with the companies. We were shipped first. No matter how hard a competitor might try to take sales away, they could never be known as, "The store that brought Finnish jackets to America." That was us!

This individual talent/competitive edge that is yours must have a value.

Let me tell you what it is **not**. It is **not** a slogan. A memorable slogan might cause customers to remember the name of your product or business — but not to buy. What benefit will I receive from buying from you? If your motel charges less because it's no-frills — **that's** a benefit. If your hamburgers are charcoal-grilled instead of fried — **that's** a benefit. If your company will let me buy gifts for Christmas and not make the first payment till **May** with no interest — **that's** a benefit. *That's competing.*

Don't try to win awards. Try to win customers. The advertising business is filled with stories of firms that win big awards but fail to deliver customers. One year Isuzu won most of the advertising awards in the industry and their sales were down 38 percent! Acura, which won few awards, sold more than any other luxury import, including Mercedes, BMW and Volvo.

Once you have an image set in your customer's mind, be careful of change. Volkswagon built a reputation on saying they had a small economical and reliable car and wound up with 67 percent of the import market. Now they advertise a big, fast expensive car and have 5 percent of the import market.

Most of all, in order to compete and come out on top, you must have the desire-to-win. Desire is just as important as natural talent or academic degrees.

A five year study of 120 of the top artists, athletes and scholars in the U.S. concluded the reason for their success was "drive and determination."

"We expected to find tales of great natural gifts," said Benjamin Bloom, a University of Chicago education professor who led the team of researchers. "But we didn't find that at all. "

Funny twist: Most of the mothers interviewed said they had **another** child more gifted than the successful ones.

There were strong similarities among the super achievers. In almost every case, parents started them off by giving them access to music, sports, learning. Most had an "independent nature" and liked to play and work alone for long periods of time.

Once the child developed a special interest, the parents were always there to help, encourage and assist. It was not unusual for parents to spend hours shuttling them to lessons.

The outstanding ones began to "live for their work" and sought out the best to help them be even better. To compete. And win.

It's a funny thing about life. If you refuse to accept anything but the best, you very often get it."
— W. Somerset Maughm

May 20, 1991, Washington Post
In Great Barrington, Mass., restaurant owner Frank Tororiello couldn't get money from banks to lease a site for his restaurant. He printed Deli dollars. Each note sold for $9 and entitled the bearer to $10 worth of food, if they waited at least six months to redeem it. "I put 500 notes on sale, and they went in a flash. Deli Dollars turned up all over town," Tortoriello said. Then, farmers put out Berkshire Farm Preserve Notes. Instead of "In God We Trust," they say "In Farms We Trust." Instead of the head of a president, they portray the head of a cabbage.

Charles A. Garfield, Berkeley psychologist picked out six characteristics of top performers:
• They are able to transcend their previous levels of accomplishment.
• They avoid the so-called comfort zone, that no-man's land where an employee feels too much at home.
• They do what they do for the art of it and are guided by compelling, internal goals.
• They solve problems rather than place blame.
• They confidently take risks after laying out the worst consequences beforehand.
• They are able to rehearse coming actions or events mentally.

INTRODUCTION TO VICTOR NIEDERHOFFER INTERVIEW
(by Neil Raphel)

I had been a lawyer and wanted desperately to quit and do something different.

Victor appeared in Atlantic City one day (he was a friend of Murray) and offered me a job. How would I like to work for his commodities firm?

When they peeled me off the ceiling, I accepted.

Six months into the job, I was discouraged. Not because of the business. The business was fascinating. And I was learning. But I felt I wasn't contributing to the firm's bottom line.

Victor walked by my desk that day. "Neil," he said, "you're doing great. Just keep reading the books on commodities trading I have given you and don't worry about contributing today. Your time will come."

Two years later, Victor promoted me to president of his firm.

Victor has an eye for the long term, for the not-obvious potential of things.

But behind his casually dressed facade beats the heart of a fierce competitor.

Victor plays to win.

He was North American squash champion for 14 consecutive years (and one-time world champion).

He built, with very little money and very large dreams, one of the most active merger and acquisition businesses in America.

And today, on the playing fields of commodities trading, Victor beats back the demons of Well-Capitalized Competitors, Market Fluctuations, and the most dangerous of all foes, Complacency.

Victor is not satisfied with his success.

And that lack of satisfaction fuels his future success.

VICTOR NIEDERHOFFER INTERVIEW
Q. How do you succeed in business when times are tough?

A. I think one has to be humble in business and always admit the possibility of failure at any time. So to answer a question about how I succeed would be vainglorious. Whenever you are overconfident, you set up the seeds of failure. I was undefeated in squash for two or three years and played a whole season without the loss of one game in the amateur ranks, and yet, before every game I always admitted the possibility I might lose **unless** I prepared for the match in the best possible way. One of my proverbs is, "Nothing recedes like success." If you don't mind, I'll question your premise in that query.

Q. Do you operate your business any differently when consumer psychology is depressed or the headlines say we're in a recession?

A. You mentioned that in a previous interview, your subject refused to even acknowledge the possibility we are in a time of weakness. I think there is a grave danger when you are in the Northeast to think that we have a monolithic economy. It's true that the financial community was decimated with the crash of October 19, 1987, and the subsequent reduction of commission income, the discrediting of investment banking operators.

Throughout the financial community there is a sense that doom has set in. And of course there is doom within their particular industry. But we have an economy that probably has five million separate business entities in 50 states, a lot of them with independent pockets. The economy is extremely diverse. The Standard Industrial Classifications has almost 100,000 different industries. And certainly within those industries there are sub-categories.

The fact is there are states doing fantastically. There are regions doing great. There are industries doing well. One of the fundamental laws of business that makes the capitalist system work is that where the rate of return is highest, business tends to seek investment. Thereby in those areas where there is the most unsatisfied demand and where resources can create the most satisfaction, resources tend to move in. It is prudent for the businessman to allocate his capital to those areas where the rate of return is highest. Furthermore, there is almost a moral imperative for businessmen to do so because that capital creates ever-increasing wealth when every asset is used most efficiently and competition works to provide customers with what they most want.

One of the things that I do at a time like the present is to allocate my resources where they have the highest return. A mistake many businesses make in difficult times is to concentrate on loss prevention and crisis management. What I've tried to with most of my businesses, most of my activities, is to be diverse enough so that they'll always be some activity where there's room for expansion, where the capital investments have good returns.

Q. I spoke to Reese Palley for this book. He's spending all his time in Romania and Russia now. Would that be a good place for a budding capitalist to go?

A. I think that is carrying it one more level. Bear in mind we've had one of the most fantastic expansions in history, perhaps the greatest peacetime expansion, maybe nine or ten years without a recession. We had an eight percent unemployment rate when President Carter left and by the end of 1990 we were at a maximum of 5.9 percent unemployment. Many of the coincident indicators had nothing but growth for eight consecutive years, almost 100 months in a row. A lot of people make the big mistake of thinking our economy is strictly the manufacturing sector. If they see the purchasing managers index of industrial production go down, they automatically assume that's the economy. It's a collectivist mistake to think that producing goods is somehow on a higher level of significance than serving goods. We have a number of areas in the service sector and in the distribution sector that are still doing very well now.

But overconfidence can be disastrous. In the business I'm mainly involved in, the speculation business, I must be ever-mindful of the possibility of failure. Unless I manage my assets prudently in terms of their variability as well as their expected return, I could be ruined. Perhaps that's another kind of subtle lesson that people should pay attention to, although in my business it is much more pronounced than others. The business person should take into account the variability of returns and the fact that even under the best of planning and circumstances events can unfold in a fashion different from anticipation. In my commodity business, an announcement can literally, at any time, bankrupt me. So if I weren't mindful of the fact that commodity prices can move 10 percent in five minutes, as they do with announcements relative to the Mideast crisis, I could certainly go under.

You brought up Reese Palley's point about recognizing opportunties. I come back to my commodities business. I cannot afford to be even swimming with the tide of the advance thinkers. I always have to be a little bit ahead of them because the commodities markets are so ingenious and subtle and they anticipate things so quickly and with such efficiency. So that while Reese Palley is talking about Russia and Eastern Europe, I gave that up about a year or two ago. I think the main opportunties right now are going to be in South America.

The tremendous prosperity, the tremendous standard of living, the material well-being and political independence and self-confidence manifested during the Reagan years provided a demonstration effect for the Eastern European countries. They looked at us as the beacon. They don't really know how things are here, but they think of us as upholding the standards of liberty. Every day they saw on television the news people talking about how Reagan is completely stupid and ineffectual and they said to themselves, "If we said that in our countries, we would go to jail. What fantastic political freedom they have! And look at the wealth that everybody has and the standards of living and their mobility." And they looked on us as the model and they saw the chaos, economic and political, that the status systems lead to and they came to think that we should be the guiding light. That they should move to a capitalist economy.

And, similarly, South America has now seen what has happened in the Eastern European countries. The countries of South America have a tradition of private property. They have dictatorships, but they also have private property. I've always said that economic freedom provides a much higher level of individual utility and satisfaction than political liberty. Of course economic liberty leads to political liberty, the two are inseparable, but when you have strong private property and an authoritarian regime, I think you have an infrastructure that can take off. As the demonstration effect spreads to South America and as the one remaining Communist society in Cuba loses all of its subsidies, as the Russians refuse to finance the last of the revolutionaries, then there could be a stampede toward democracy and economic freedom in South America. I'm very much looking forward to that as a new frontier, even more so than Eastern Europe.

Q. From a microeconomic point of view, is an individual well-advised to invest in businesses that he or she knows well?

A. I think I've been pretty good about creating incentives at the companies that I'm associated with where the my success was intimately related to the success of others. In every situation I've been associated with I've provided a strong equity or profit center for all my colleagues. I think the idea of running all your enterprises in a centralized business where you somehow feel that you have all the answers does not work. That can only be effective in your own business where you know it intimately.

Q. So you invest in people more than businesses?

A. I try to find businesses that have a high return and in areas with the right trends and try to people them with good incentives. I think that it's the system that makes the individual. There is nobody more entrepreneurial or more able than the African farmer. In fact, in South Africa in the early 1900s, the African farmers were competing extremely effectively with the Dutch and the English. It was because of that, that all the apartheid laws were developed in an attempt by the establishment to prevent the enterprise structure from allowing those who weren't already part of the structure to advance.

The point of this is that if you have a profit system, than you will create good people. They will rise.

Q. Is there a direct connection between your success in athletics and your success in business? What qualities that you use to compete in sports have you used for success in business?

A. Francis Galton in his epic study of eminence advanced the theory that there are four qualities of success that are common to every field. Galton studied the 200 most eminent people throughout world history and he concluded that they all had four characteristics in common.

The first quality was what he called "powers of organizations," approaching life in a systematic fashion.

I've always been very systematic. I just played you a game of chess in which you beat me. But I took down the scorecard to show someone who has the ability to help me understand my mistakes. I'll try to improve. I'll study what I did wrong. Every eminent person that Galton studied was very systematic and organized — "businesslike" he called it. That was his first quality of success, having a businesslike attitude.

I became systematic from my study of the piano as a child. When I approached the game of squash, I broke down the game into all of its most elementary parts. I used to take a book onto the court. I had never played squash before I started. I took a book out and I was looking at all the pictures in the book and trying to hit the same strokes as the pictures. My coach came up to me and said, "Don't you know you're playing the wrong game. That's a book on English squash. That's completely different than American squash. All the strokes are completely cockeyed. That book was written in 1890." I still have it.

I practiced against myself constantly. Very few squash players have done that. I came out on the court and I would break down the game into its component parts and practice against myself. I would practice each shot individually. From the piano you know you certainly have to play the scales first. You have to play the right hand separately from the left hand. You have to write down the areas where you make the mistakes and then practice those individually. Hardly anyone else ever did that in squash. All my teammates, my competitors, they played games against **each other**. I had a much better method — I practiced against myself — a systematic, businesslike approach.

In my commodities business we have an overall view, but for every hour of every day we have a systematic set of business procedures of what to follow. Our pattern program, which tries to find opportunities for speculating in the markets, now has more than a million lines of code in it. We have our commodities business extremely systematized. I'm very proud of that operation. I think that's the greatest feat of my career. We have a grand idea that permeates everything we do. We have it extremely systematized.

The second quality Galton mentioned in his four characteristics of success was "persistence." That is the quality that marks me to the highest degree. I don't think there is anyone I have to take much of a back seat to in the area of persistence. When I was playing squash, I think I played 365 days a year for 20 years straight. I once calculated I had played in more than 10,000 separate tournament matches.

When I play the piano, I play every day. My greatest successes in business have come from supplying a little bit extra work, staying up until eleven or twelve o'clock to put a little extra effort into a project and sticking with something, coming at it a different way. Recently we developed a new idea for commodities markets which I am quite excited about. It came from approaching the same subject many different ways. We finally came up with the idea that it was relative movements of commodities that was much more important than absolute individual movements. It's a small variation on our idea of interdependence of markets, but it may have been literally the 200th kind of approach we've come up with under this general rubric. So persistence is very important. And I think you'd find that in almost every successful person.

The third quality that Galton mentioned for the eminent people was good health. By this he meant the ability to work. Not that they had to be in good physical health, but they had to have a good mental health. They couldn't be sickly. In general, they had to live a long life without spending too much time as an invalid or worrying about their own ability to get a job done. Good health is very important to me. I remember once in my squash career, one of my coaches said to me, "You know everybody talks about the fact that your opponents are such great athletes and you're such a plodder. But one thing I've noticed after watching you for 16 or 17 years, I've never seen you injured once. Everybody else has bad arms, bad eyes, bad knees or they have all the bandages. I never see you with a bandage." And wouldn't you know, a week later my career basically ended when I sprained my ankle and I didn't fix it for three years. But, in general, I was very good about taking care of my health. And since that time I've been very effective in terms of living a life that is consistent with good health.

I exercise every day. I doubt that there have been more that four or five days since I've been one year old that I haven't spent doing at least fifteen to twenty minutes of aerobic exercise. I also follow some of the principles of longevity that I've learned from books. I try to eat things that are going to be digested quickly and efficiently.

I follow the precepts one of my seven most favorite books in the world called "The Conquest of Cancer." The author has deep insights into the way that the forces of the world are moving. After reading that book, I haven't had a drop of chicken and have a diet consisting mainly of fish and vegetables. Our kids do also. In so doing I've managed to stave off the ravages of old age to a reasonable degree.

Galton's final characteristic is what he calls a "modicum of ability," which others would call "the flash of genius" or "the creative spark" but what I'd rather call an "idee fixe." It's some general overview of what your mission is and a dogged pursuit of that mission. Something that differentiates you, that provides the culture and the organizational principles for your activities. In my commodities business I came up with that idea that all markets all over the world are completely interrelated with predicable lead patterns. That was a very good idea — it was a rich idea — it was much richer than 99.9 percent of the ideas of our competitors. Our competitors believed that individual markets moved in statistically predicable ways that could be predicted through analysis. Our idea opened up vast new territory. Whether it was correct or not still remains to be seen. But you certainly have to have a good idea to succeed.

So those four qualities would summarize the rules to success in good times as well as bad times.

Fortunately, in my business, which is speculation, there is no reason that a strong economy or a weak economy should be unusually good or bad for me. I'm trying to project where things are going to be in the future and to help move prices and supply and demand to where they are more likely to be when equilibrium gets restored. And whether equilibrium gets restored on the bullish or bearish side is a matter of supreme indifference to me. The only thing that really should be totally disastrous to me is if there is a sustained move that becomes reflexively reinforcing.

SURVIVE!

SURVIVE! INTRODUCTION

"Survive!" is the final chapter of this book. But it may also be the most important. When times seem most bleak, "tough selling" becomes most important.

In fact, I have a theory about business.

It goes like this:

If I'm doing business in my town it's not because of the weather, the time of the year or the economy. It's me. I'm doing something **right**.

And . . . if I'm **not doing** business in my town, it's not because of the weather, the time of the year or the economy — it's me. I'm doing something **wrong**.

After all, somebody's buying something from someone!

Now, how am I going to have them buy from me?

SURVIVE! QUOTES

"If you keep on saying things are going to be bad, you have a good chance of being a prophet" — **Isaac Singer**

"Ya hafta earn what ya get."— **Little Orphan Annie**

AGE BEFORE BEAUTY

Many people believe that they can't make the changes necessary to achieve their goals. Many people who are fifty, forty, thirty, sometimes even twenty, think "If only I had done (fill in the blank for your personal regret) earlier. It's too late now."

Wrong!

It is never too late to try something "different" — You are not the first, nor will you be the last, to find success elusive.

And your success has little, if anything, to do with your age.

Here are some examples:

• Othmar Ammann retired at 60 and **then** designed the Connecticut and New Jersey Turnpikes, the Pittsburgh Civic Arena, Dulles Airport, The Throgs Neck Bridge, the Verrazano Narrows Bridge.

• Churchill retired and started writing and won the Nobel Prize at 79.

• Vanderbilt constructed most of his railroads when he was over 70.

• Walter Damrosch wrote one of the greatest operas at 75.

• Monet was still painting at 86.

• Goethe wrote the second part of "Faust" when he was 80.

• Victor Hugo produced his famous "Torquemada" at 80.

• Titian painted the famous "Battle of Lepanto" at 98.

• Verdi wrote his greatest opera, "Otello" at 74. And followed that with "Falstaff" at 80!

And then there's the story of the cook at a roadside cafe who had failed in selling insurance, running a ferryboat, and a gas station. The state bought the location of his restaurant for a superhighway. Now he was 66 and went on Social Security drawing $108 a month. Looking for ways to increase his income, he worked as a part time cook in local restaurants and was known for his famous fried chicken. He made an arrangement with restaurants who wanted to know his "secret recipes". He said he'd give it to them if they gave him 5 cents on every chicken they cooked with his formula. They agreed.

He was so successful in selling the chicken concept to other people that in just five years he had 400 franchises. He sold out to John Brown, former governor of Kentucky, for $2 million and a guarantee of a job for the rest of his life (he didn't want to go back on Social Security).

At age 88 he said he had three goals:

1. "I want to live to be 100."

2. "At that time I'll take off two years because I haven't had a vacation since I cooked that first piece of chicken and I'm getting tired."

3. "After that vacation, I want to come back with another new idea."

He didn't quite make it. Died in his 90's but will always be remembered with his face on the front of the largest fast food chain in the world: Colonel Harlan Sanders, Mr. Kentucky Fried Chicken.

Today there are more than 8,000 franchises in 58 countries with more than $5 billion in annual sales. All begun by a man who started when he was 66 years old.

TELLING YOUR STORY

Part of surviving is to constantly tell everyone who you are, what you do and where you do it. Such announcements are necessary because the world is constantly changing.

Consider this fact: In the town in which you live, 20 percent of the people change their address every year.

Some are born. Some die. Some move in. Some move out. But one of out of five addresses change every year and are you still walking around saying "Everyone knows who I am and what I do!" Don't believe it. Otherwise why are all those national manufacturers with well recognized brand names spending nearly $1 million for a 30 second spot on the Super Bowl? They want people to know they are still in business in the same stand.

You must be persistent in telling people about your business. Yet, persistency is a trait shared by few. One of the most quoted statements on this theme is from Calvin Coolidge. As President of the United States he was best known for his taciturn image. A woman once approached him at a party and said, "President Coolidge, I just made a bet with my husband that I can make you say more than three words."

Coolidge looked at her and said, "You lose."

But his thoughts on persistence are found in most books of Quotations. Here's what he said:

"Nothing in the world can take the place of persistence. Talent will not. Nothing is more common than unsuccessful men with talent. Genius will not. Unrewarded genius is almost a proverb. Education will not. The world is full of educated derelicts. Persistence and determination alone are omnipotent."

You have to constantly tell your story. Why do so many companies cut back on their advertising when Times Are Tough? It should be the time you spend **more** on advertising. Because there are those out there who do not know, who never knew and will never know unless you constantly tell them. And if you forget to remind your customers about who you are and what you do, your customers will simply stop coming back.

CUSTOMERS WHO DON'T COME BACK

A major research company did a survey of why people stopped shopping where they used to shop. These are the results.

Fourteen percent left because of complaints that were not taken care of.

Nine percent left because of the competition.

Nine percent left because they moved.

Sixty-eight percent left because of . . . no special reason.

In other words, nearly seven out of 10 customers who left your business leave for no special reason.

I don't believe that. I think there is a reason.

They left because you didn't tell them you cared.

They left because you didn't keep in touch.

They left because you took them for granted.

And yet, it is far, far easier to sell more to the customer you have than to sell a new customer.

The easiest, least complicated and most effective way to not only keep your customer but also keep them coming back is to let the customer **know** you care.

One way: the way you treat them in your business.

The other way: to transfer this service to your mailbox.

For the price of a postage stamp you can clone yourself and arrive in your customers' (and yes, potential customers') mailboxes all over your community.

Now you have one-on-one uncompetitive selling relationships.

Now you have a chance to tell/sell your message.

Now you have an opportunity to not only have your customer return but, as important, to make sure they do not leave.

Fourteen Percent Left Because Of Complaints Not Taken Care Of

"The best companies invest in complaints," says Richard

Whitley, president of a Boston consulting firm. "They actively search out their unhappy consumers: that's giving them even **more** than they expected."

It's not easy to keep customers happy. The larger you grow, the more difficult the problem. L.L. Bean, the mail order sportswear company in Maine, was growing at double digit rates for several years, then abruptly canceled plans for their new warehouse and cut back on mailing to new lists. Here's why: The merchandise being returned had climbed to 14 percent a year, costing Bean about $80 million a year!

They decided to consolidate, take care of their existing problems, make their present customers happy before looking for new ones.

Maytag washers ran a campaign for years showing that their repairman fell asleep all day in his office because no one called to complain. Now that's an image to inspire confidence.

Nine Percent Left Because Of The Competition

The department store was always the prime source for consumer spending around the world. But many of the leading department store chains in the country are bankrupt or out of buesiness. Peter Solomon, investment banker, says, "Department stores are at the end of their life cycle and have to be reinvented."

What is that reinvention?

Here's one suggestion from Talbot's, a company that began as a mail order clothier and now has a chain of retail stores: "We have to go back to the way it was when families and independent operators ran the store — customer service."

The U.S. Department Store Graveyard has seen a lot of new tombstones. Those that died: B. Altman, Best & Company, Gimbels, Frost Brothers, Joske's and Bonwit Teller. Running a high fever are such famous stores as Bloomingdale's, Saks Fifth Avenue and Marshall Field.

Said Stanley Marcus, whose father founded the famous Neiman-Marcus department store: "Unless department stores can adjust prices or improve services there may not be any place for them."

His store has done just that with their "InCircle" club. Charge customers are automatically credited with InCircle points each month giving them special privileges, benefits and rewards.

But look, there, on the horizon, riding down from the northwestern part of the United States is a . . . can it be? . . . yes . . . a department store!

Their name: Nordstrom

Their story: Success

Their reason: Service

When they arrived in the overstored California market from their home base in Seattle, Washington, the competition said, "They can't succeed."

But they did. And marched from San Francisco (opening day: $1.7 million) to Los Angeles, then hopscotched across the United States. Today they have 59 stores in six states doing $2.3 billion in sales.

Nordstrom customers are converted zealots. They proselytize. They preach the gospel of happiness, contentment and encourage others to join the faith.

What does this one store do that others do not?

Take care of the customer.

The stories are legendary:

"Did you know in Alaska they go to the customer's car and start it so it will be warm when the customer finishes shopping?"

"Did you hear the story of the customer that brought four tires in for a refund to the Seattle store. He received a refund. But the store doesn't sell tires!"

"When you walk in the store, someone offers to check your packages, suitcases and coats. **Free.**"

"They call a taxi if you need one and stay there until it comes."

"If you ask for the pay phone, they tell you to use their phone. Free."

What are they doing? **Business!**

Here's what a rival store buyer said. "Nordstrom tells everyone that works there, the customer is the most important person that walks through the door. It's not the buyer. It's not the management. It's the customer."

When you buy a product, **your** salesperson suggests tie-ins to other departments. **Your** salesperson **takes you** to the other department and continues the sale themselves. No pointed finger giving directions, "What you want is over there." The salesperson **takes you** "over there." And sells you.

Motivational speaker Brian Tracy says 80 percent of a sale is attitude and personality and only 20 percent of a sale is the quality of product.

That makes sense. No matter how high the quality of what you are selling, your **attitude** is what your customer sees, hears, experiences **first**. That's the reason for the success of the salespeople in Nordstrom's. They understand that 80 percent of the purchase depends on how they treat the customer.

"We don't want to talk about our service," says Bruce Nordstrom, co-chairman. "We are not as good as our reputation. It is a very fragile thing. You just have to do it every time, every day."

Is this much different than the mailing piece that goes to the home of your customer? Maintain a relationship with them and they will **not** be one of the 9 percent that goes to the competition, they will come back. And come back. And come back.

Nine Percent Left Because They Moved

General Electric's "Answer Service" follows the customer wherever they go with their 800 telephone number. No matter where you buy a General Electric product in the United States, you can call their toll-free number if you have any problems. And so General Electric becomes not just the store in your hometown, they become available to you wherever you go. In touch with you through telemarketing their products when you call for advice and/or problem solving.

Sixty-Eight Percent Left For No Special Reason

How do you reward your loyal customers? To ignore them is to have seven out of 10 leave "for no special reason."

One of the first to say "thank you" to their steady customers was the airline industry with their Frequent Flyer programs. Their best customers received bonus points for miles traveled for future free travel. Other stores and businesses saw the results and formed a me-too parade.

The hotel industry came first with Holiday Inns. Marriott began their program in November 1983. Today they have 3 million members. The program was so successful that other hotel chains had to match their program. Said Adam Aron, marketing vice president of the Hyatt chain, "From 1983 to 1986 the hotel industry was losing so much business to Marriott we **had** to match them." (see "Reward!" chapter)

The average supermarket shopper spends about a quarter million dollars while food shopping in their lifetime. Until now, no store has ever bothered to say "thank you" except for a perfunctory remark as the customer leaves. One reason why: The average supermarket has nearly 10,000 customers shopping the store every week. You simply can't keep track of them mentally. But many of today's supermarkets now keep track of them electronically. And give them rewards for shopping the store.

It's about time.

In today's tough retail environment, you need to keep in touch with your customers. If you do, you will not only bring in new customers, you will bring back the ones that left for some reason to the competitive jungle.

ONCE YOU COMMIT TO CHANGE, COMMIT ALL THE WAY OR YOU WILL SIMPLY REPEAT YOUR MISTAKES

After World War I, a great cholera epidemic struck the Orient. Thousands of people were dying in India, Burma — but not in China. Doctors investigated and discovered the cholera germ came through the drinking of water. Since the Chinese drank tea, the water was boiled, and the cholera germ was destroyed.

Quick, tell the people to boil their water!

Everyone said they were obeying the doctor's prescriptions but the disease kept on spreading. Finally the doctors discovered the reason why: The population thought the boiling of water was a prescription and they were only taking a few drops a day. And continuing to drink the water!

You can't make changes by drops. You must quit cold turkey when what you are doing is **not** working and try something else.

TRY SOMETHING NEW

Finally, if you are not happy in your business, don't despair. Try something new. Answer the question: "If you had to do it all over, what would you **rather** do than what you're doing now?"

Here's some who decided they'd rather switch than fight:
- Conrad Hilton began as a banker.
- George Washington thought he'd make a living as a surveyor.
- Somerset Maugham was a doctor.
- Paul Gauguin was a stockbroker before trying his hand at painting.
- Norman Vincent Peale was a newspaperman.
- Albert Schweitzer was a musician.
- St. Peter began as a fisherman.

People can and **do** change.

Consider the story of the Nine Famous Irishmen.

In the Irish rebellion in 1848, the following nine men were captured, tried and convicted of treason against her Majesty the Queen and sentenced to death: John Mitchell, Morris Lyene, Pat Donahue, Thomas McGee, Charles Duffy, Thomas Meagher, Richard O'Gorman, Terrence McManus, Michael Ireland.

Before passing sentence the judge asked if there was anything any of them wished to say. Meagher, speaker for them all, said,

"My Lord, this is our first offense but not our last. If you will be easy with us this time, we promise on our word as gentlemen to try to do better next time. And next time, sure, we won't be fools enough to get caught."

The indignant judge ordered them all to be hanged by the neck until dead and drawn and quartered. Passionate protests from all over the world forced Queen Victoria to commute the sentences to exile for life to far off Australia.

In 1874, 25 years later, word reached Queen Victoria that Sir Charles Duffy, elected Prime Minister of Australia, was the same Charles Duffy she sent there 25 years ago. On the Queen's request, the records of the rest of the convicts were brought to her:

Thomas Francis Meagher was the Governor of Montana in the U.S.

Terrence McManus and Patrick Donahue were both Brigadier Generals in the U.S. Army.

Richard O'Gorman was Governor General of Newfoundland.

Morris Lyene was the Attorney General of Australia.

Michael Ireland succeeded him in that office.

Thomas McGee was a member of the Canadian Parliament, Minister of Agriculture and President of Council of the Dominion of Canada.

John Mitchell was a prominent politician in New York City.

So, do not worry not because you think you are locked into what you are doing.

Because you are not.

And, most of all, do **not** spend your creative hours worrying over what the competition is doing. Worry about what **you** are doing. Make them pick up the paper or listen to the radio and watch your store because they're concerned about what you will do next.

Above all: Never be bitter or mad with anyone. Try this: Don't try to get even with anybody unless they have done something good for you.

EDDY BOAS INTRODUCTION

"Survive!" is such an important chapter that we decided to end it with two interviews. And if **anyone** belongs in the chapter under "Survive!" it is Eddy Boas. Now president of Dun and Bradstreet's subsidiary, I.M.S. Direct Marketing Division, he travels around the world as their trouble shooter making sure the various companies he visits not only "survive" but also succeed.

Eddy's instincts for survival started early. He was two years old when he was taken with his family to the Nazi concentration camp in Bergen-Belsen.

EDDY BOAS INTERVIEW

Q. Tell us about your war experience.

A. As far as I know, my family is the only one that went into a German concentration camp as a family and came out together as a family. My father was in the Dutch army. When they were defeated, they sent my mother, father, myself and my brother to the Bergen-Belsen concentration camp in Germany — the same camp where Anne Frank was with her family. I was only two years old. When the Allies were approaching, the Germans put us on a train going to the East toward the gas chambers. The allies were bombing the railway tracks and the train stalled.

After being on the train for 17 days with no food, we were captured by Russians in April, 1945, close to the Czechoslovakia border. We were taken to Risa in East Germany. We escaped from the Russians, walked for some days and came to River Elbe, where we were again taken by Russians who thought we were French. We were swapped to the Americans for four gypsies. The Americans sent us to the British who sent us to Holland in May, 1945.

My father died in 1948 from injuries in the concentration camp. I was eight years old and my mother was able to get one of the first visas after the war to Australia.

Q. Why Australia?

A. My mother wanted to get as far away from Europe as possible.
We did have some distant relatives there. But it was difficult.
Talk about survival — none of us could speak English! So my
mother went to work as a cleaning lady. I went to vocational
school. To survive I had to learn English quickly. I left school at
fifteen to bring money into the house and got a job cleaning out
factories for about two dollars a week. I learned a lesson: You can
always find work if you're really willing to work. I also caddied
at the local golf courses for a dollar a day. I left there to be a radio
station panel operator for six years. I was earning $22 a week but
wasn't learning much. Then I met a friend who was making
about $50 a week as a salesman. "Say," I said, "that's what I
should be — a salesman!"

I quickly learned there are two things you must do to be a good
salesperson if you want to survive:

1. Believe in your product. If you don't believe in it, you can't
sell it.

2. Make enough calls. If you don't make enough calls, it
doesn't matter how good you are. You could be the best salesman
in the world. But you have to play the percentages to do well.

I made some good money and took off for Europe and spent all
my savings in one year. I returned to Australia, got married and
thought I should come to North America to earn big money.
Came to Canada. Got a job selling office supplies and was their
number two salesman in Canada the first year!

Q. How long were you in Canada?

A. Only about a year. I missed Australia. I came back and
worked for another office equipment company. I worked day and
night. I did very well but in 1974 there was a depression in
Australia and the company went broke. The building we were in
was owned by a mailing company called Permail. I told them I
was leaving because the company went out of business. The

owner asked me what I was doing and I told him, "Trying to survive." I had a wife, two small babies and three mortgages. He said, "Why don't you come and sell direct mail for me."

I said "Sure," even though I didn't know the meaning of the words "direct mail."

That was in January 1975. I built Permail into one of the largest mailing houses in Australia. And I found out why I liked direct mail so much: It's just like being a salesman. The mailing list is the salesman calling on the territory. The envelope is the clothing the salesman wears. If the customer doesn't open the message, it doesn't matter how creative the message is inside. It's like a salesman who visits a client wearing shorts and a dirty t-shirt. He won't get past the secretary to see the buyer.

Q. What type of direct mail does Permail do?

A. Packages and letters for Australian companies mainly in the pharmaceutical industry. We receive the finished packages from advertising agencies and mail them. We wound up having the only exclusive accurate list of all the doctors in Australia.

Q. But now you're no longer a salesman on your own. You're hiring salespeople. What's your criteria?

A. Personality. How enthusiastic are they? Do they look you in the eye. Do they have self confidence. Are they hungry? Not for food — but for success. Remember, I never had a higher education but I had a better one — working the streets. Being streetwise is more important than having a degree. When I started with Permail there were 40 employees. Today there are 120. After I hire them, I let them do their own thing. Make their own decisions. The problem with a lot of senior managers is they don't let their staff make decisions. I don't know how the laser printer works. I don't know much about computers. I still use a typewriter and a calculator. What I do best is to simply be . . . a salesman.

Q. *So if your staff says, "We should buy this computer," you say . . .*

A. "Buy it." Either you have faith in your staff or they shouldn't be working for you.

Q. *Since we're talking about survival, your company sent you to manage one of their operations in New Jersey. It was on the road to failure. How did you make it survive?*

A. It wasn't easy. I had to immediately fire about 50 people. Since we had three hundred people that meant nearly 20 percent were let go when I first arrived! But I told myself, and anyone who would listen, if we don't let those 50 go, then all 300 go.

Q. *How did you decide who stayed and who left?*

A. I didn't decide. The staff decided. I had the managers rate everyone from one to ten. Weren't many tens. Lots of fours and fives. Managers don't like to make those decisions. But I told them if they wanted the company to remain and their jobs to stay, that's their job.

Q. *You were then given the same responsibility for a company in England.*

A. It wasn't easy there, either. But you keep an eye on the ultimate goal: Survive and succeed. With the thinned down staff you have to have them motivated. You tell them they are the survivors because they are. Their job is secure. I talked to every single person in the company. I believe in open door management. I worked on the floor with the people on the machines. I showed them we were a team. You motivate by example. They're working hard. I'm working hard. And most of all, I like to do what I do best: sell. When the sales force wants someone to go out with them to a difficult client, I go because I love it.

Q. Tell us about your Pan Pacific Direct Marketing Seminar in Australia. This is the largest marketing conference of its kind in the Pacific Rim. How did it happen?

A. I was running a successful direct marketing program for Permail Pty. Ltd. with the Canadian Olympics. They invited me to the Olympics in Montreal. I went and met Larry Chait, one of the gurus in Direct Marketing and Pete Hoke, publisher of Direct Marketing magazine. They said that direct marketing was the advertising of the future and asked, "Why don't you run a seminar in Australia on direct mail?"

No one ever did that before. I did the first one in 1977 and the only speaker was Larry Chait. We had 30 people in the audience. Everyone said I should stop. It couldn't succeed. They didn't know I was a survivor. I just had to find out how to do it right. So the next year I went to the International Direct Marketing Symposium in Montreux, Switzerland. I saw how the program should be put together and came back to Australia and ran it as a direct mail show for the next three years. After that we expanded to all forms of direct marketing: telephone, electronic, print. Today we have a show and exhibition that attracts 3,000 people. We also became the first people to put a direct marketing program together for New Zealand and Asia.

Q. Haven't other people seen your success and tried to compete with you?

A. Yes. And they failed.

Q. Why?

A. It's the drive we put into it. It's simply . . .hard work and the belief you can survive. And succeed.

Q. How do you motivate yourself?

A. Ego. You get up in the morning and say, "I can hardly wait to get to work!"

Q. *What about the recession. What about tough economic times?*

A. There's no such thing. The country may be in a recession but that doesn't mean your business is in a recession. It's not a problem. It's an opportunity. I just have to go out and knock on more doors than before. Selling direct mail is great because you can immediately see if the campaign works or doesn't work.

Q. *Final question: While we're talking today, the U.S. is having a difficult time economically. Australia is having an even more difficult time. How can a business survive?*

A.You have to be more aggressive in Australia because we have a smaller population. Our country is about the same physical size as the U.S., with only a fraction of the population. In the U.S. people tend to sit back and wait for things to happen. That wasn't true when the U.S. was younger. There were a lot of entrepreneurs then because they were willing to work hard to survive. Today you don't find a lot of those people around. They may want to survive. But they don't know how. It's not difficult. It's two words: **Work Hard**.

ERIC LUTZ INTRODUCTION

Eric Lutz is a good friend who has seen and taken part in the good and bad times in the real estate industry. We admire Eric Lutz for his imagination, his hard work, his attention to detail and his ability to survive.

Eric has had more than his share of successes. He converted hundreds of run-of-the-mill apartment units into attractive condominiums by adding important amenities such as attractive landscaping, recreational facilities and interior fix-up. He has built office buildings and hotels. He grew from a one-man operation into a 500-person organization and, with Eric's financial genius, he has made money for scores of investors. Eric's projects are first class, and he is very well regarded in the real estate community.

Recently, Eric had problems when a savings and loan which was financing a major hotel project of his folded. Eric had problems working with the Resolution Trust Corporation, the government agency in charge of the savings and loan bailout, and suffered major losses in the project.

So Eric had to take drastic steps to insure his business survival. Here are some thoughts about his personal troubles and the ability to survive during difficult times.

ERIC LUTZ INTERVIEW

Q. Tell us about the troubles you had with a loan on your hotel.

A. In this particular case the loan was a five year loan. There was six months left on the loan, and we asked the two S & L's, one of which was a joint venture partner, that they extend the loan and lower the interest because interest rates had dropped. Both of the loan participants agreed, and then they went bankrupt. The RTC took control. Political policy rather than practicality became the new measurement, and so they made a decision they would not modify any loans or extend any loans. They demanded immediate payment for the 15 million dollar loan. Given the weak credit markets and the fact that the hotel had just been renovated, it was not in a position to support any new loans. Therefore we gave the hotel to the RTC and paid them one million dollars which I had to raise in one week. We conveyed the hotel to be relieved of any personal liability.

When I realized that the government had taken over and they did not act as a normal private banker would, I began to prepare what I thought would be the worst case scenario. It has evolved in the last two year period. I borrowed the million dollars that was needed to pay the RTC from partners who had become friends. These people thought enough of me to help me. I took my equity assets and secured them against loans that had been advanced. I took a poison pill. If any lender or creditor tried to take advantage of my lack of liquidity or weakened financial position, I would be able to say, "If you push me you will gain nothing because all of my assets will be transferred and put in the hands of friendly creditors."

It took me twenty-eight years to build a real estate empire, consisting of 53 buildings, during which time I had never been in a court of law. There were never any losses in any landlord-tenant lawsuit or a condominium lawsuit. I find myself now in the middle of real estate travesties of the late 80s and early 90s which have been compounded by the fact that the U.S. government was not only the largest owner of real estate but also the largest financial institution and created a credit crunch.

I worked to dismantle, in a 18 month period, that which took 28 years to build up. I sold approximately $85 million worth of real estate to try to position myself to withstand what I perceived to be the circumstances that could occur. I reduced my organization from 500 people down to 50 people. I was forced to face a new set of experiences. I had to face failure, had to manage liabilities, had to be confronted with adverse publicity, had to manage with great effort any negative emotional feelings which I have thought would have an adverse effect on my own efforts.

Q. Did this occur because you were in the real estate business which involves a lot of leverage?

A. No. The mortgages on my real estate only represent 65 percent of the property value based upon the current low valuation. Some of my friends are losing building after building to lenders. I'm not experiencing that. I didn't have the problem of over-leverage. But as you talk to me this day, I am an individual who is fighting for his business survival, his financial survival and certainly I am fighting for my emotional survival. It is difficult to make the distinction but it is important that I don't act based upon the wrong emotional set of feelings.

Q. Are you at this point bitter about your experience? There seems to be a certain edge when you talk about the RTC and what the government did.

A. I made a decision early that such thoughts would be counter-productive. I do experience anxiety. But that is anxiety about meeting my obligation. That is a heavy burden.

Q. Do you still have the same feelings about real estate that you once did?

A. It is very interesting. You made reference to my enthusiasm, the things I love to do with real estate of a creative nature. I have used my imagination to develop appropriate strategies and business plans to engineer myself and my business through this very unusual set of circumstances. You're speaking to a man who lost many millions of dollars. I have taken enthusiasm and imagination and employed it in a different form and fashion — to develop a defensive plan.

We are going forward to do new things. Number one: Make an accurate self-assessment of my circumstances. If an individual is going to accomplish his or her goals, then he or she must exert leadership over their self if not others. That means making an accurate assessment of your strengths and weaknesses, as well as the circumstances you face. I also believe that an individual's greatest strength is that individual's greatest potential weakness.

In my own case, my strength was my imagination and sensitivity to other people. My greatest potential weakness is the same.

My sensitivity to people served me well in having relationships, but when you're dealing with adversity one needs to be tough. I have difficulty in being tough with other people because of my sensitivity. We had to first minimize our losses. We did that.

Number two: Hold on to existing real estate and through extensive merchandising and market programs out-perform the market. We used our imagination to develop a strategy to take advantage of the existing market condition. In the last six months we formed two new joint venture partners. One to pursue the development of facilities of American companies expanding both nationally and internationally based upon the changes in Europe in 1992. Major corporations need plants. We have a world wide corporation with the capacity to build plants throughout the world. We are currently negotiating to buy one of the largest management companies in the US out of bankruptcy. We are negotiating to buy real estate from insurance companies, banks and savings who have foreclosed on properties and will loan 80 percent of the money necessary to buy the asset.

We have shrunk our base in a realistic manner which is a very humbling experience. You have to set aside any ego because if you have one you will not survive the adversity.

Q. Anything that you would say to someone first starting out? What would you say are the things that they should be looking out for?

A. They have to take three jobs.

The first job: Work for an organization where they will learn the most.

The second job: Earn the most.

The third job: Have the most fun. In that order!

Also important: I have noticed that those individuals who write out or schedule the things that they are going to do and list their daily and weekly activities are the ones that generally succeed. They set up expectations on a daily basis. When they meet and complete their goals they generally progress forward and have a sense of accomplishment.

Failure usually occurs because individuals set expectations too low or unrealistically too high. When they don't meet those expectations they give up. The tenacious people are usually well-organized and set up expectations and work hard to meet them.

Q. What is your view of the future? Are you optimistic?

A. There is a greater opportunity today than there ever was. In the field of real estate, it may have been over-valued and littered more than it should have in the late 80s. As we speak, the general consumer has a negative view of real estate which is misplaced. It has historically been an area where wealth was accumulated. It was only during the 1980s that so much money was attracted into real estate that it became a trinket of Wall Street. As a result, capital became cheap and profits were made by syndicators in Wall Street. In the 1980s real estate was following the pattern of every declining industry. The profit was not made in the ownership of real estate. It was made because of perceived future value. When real estate returns to the hands and ownership of professionals who are emotionally committed, who have the knowledge to operate, it will succeed and prosper. There are more opportunities today in real estate than has been the case since World War II.

CONCLUSION

Every business person needs a "kitchen cabinet."

No, we're not talking about home remodeling. In the sense we're using it, "kitchen cabinet" began as a political phrase, referring to the unpaid and untitled friends and advisors surrounding President Franklin Roosevelt.

Roosevelt turned to his "kitchen cabinet" whenever he needed straight-from-the-gut advice, advice untempered by personal agendas. Roosevelt knew that the members of his "kitchen cabinet" were looking out for his best interests.

Similarly, the businessmen profiled and interviewed in this book are our "kitchen cabinet." When we're feeling low and we need a kick in the pants, we conjure up Stew Leonard. Just picturing Stew's enthusiasm inspires us to tackle our next project and the word "Wow!" springs excitedly from our lips.

Thinking of Victor Niederhoffer makes us want to "Compete!," vanquish any foe. Joe Sugarman reminds us to "Listen!" to our customers and Sol Price reminds us to "Help!"

We hope you use the stories, anecdotes, profiles and interviews in this book as your own "kitchen cabinet." The principles of business success outlined in this book are not difficult to understand or put into practice. And, best of all, they are habit forming.

If you start practicing the principles of customer service outlined in these pages, you'll begin to notice more and more smiles on the people you wait on and work with. Since enthusiasm is contagious, the people around you will begin to mimic your upbeat attitudes. The more you organize your time, the more time you'll find to concentrate on your special, unique talents.

We hope the principles in this book help you solve the "tough times" that block the way to achieving your business goals.

Your opportunity for business success is in your hands.

Murray and Neil Raphel
Atlantic City, New Jersey
November, 1991